MY CHAINS FELL OFF

William Wells Brown, Fugitive Abolitionist

L.H. Whelchel, Jr.

UNIVERSITY
PRESS OF
AMERICA

LANHAM • NEW YORK • LONDON

Copyright © 1985 by

University Press of America,™ Inc.

4720 Boston Way
Lanham, MD 20706

3 Henrietta Street
London WC2E 8LU England

All rights reserved

Printed in the United States of America

All University Press of America books are produced on acid-free
paper which exceeds the minimum standards set by the National
Historical Publications and Records Commission.

Library of Congress Cataloging in Publication Data

Whelchel, L.H.
  My chains fell off.

  Bibliography: p.
  Includes index.
  1. Brown, William Wells, 1815-1884. 2. Fugitive
slaves—United States—Biography. 3. Abolitionists—
United States—Biography. 4. Afro-Americans—Biography.
5. Slavery—United States—Anti-slavery movements.
I. Title.
E450.B883W44   1984   305.5'67'0924 [B]   84-21027
ISBN 0-8191-4367-7 (alk. paper)
ISBN 0-8191-4368-5 (pbk. : alk. paper)

Acknowledgements

I am deeply indebted in the writing of this work to Paine College, Boston University School of Theology, New York University, Duke University, and Miles College.

I am grateful to Metropolitan Christian Methodist Episcopal Church in Birmingham, Alabama, Russell Memorial Christian Methodist Episcopal Church, Durham, North Carolina, and Phillips Temple Christian Methodist Episcopal Church, Dayton, Ohio.

To numerous libraries I am indebted for use of manuscripts and other resources.

I am grateful to Dr. Stuart C. Henry, professor of American Christianity, for his encouragement and helpful criticisms. To Dr. William Edward Farrison I am indebted for the use of his works on William Wells Brown.

I am grateful to University of Chicago Press, Harper and Row, and other publishers for permission to reprint in this book portions of material originally published in their books and journals.

I also wish to thank my research assistant, secretary, my teachers, students and family for encouragement, assistance and advice at critical stages in the development of this manuscript.

November 1982
LHW

TABLE OF CONTENTS

	Introduction	ix
I	Sandford's Lot	1
II	A Strange and Cruel Democracy	10
III	William Wells	15
IV	Freedom	18
V	The Call to Battle	26
VI	A Mighty Pen	45
VII	High Propaganda	51
VIII	The Color of Ham and Cain	63
IX	Conclusion	67
	Notes	83
	Bibliography	93
	Index	113
	Author's Biographical Note	

"When I alone thought myself lost,
My dungeon shook, my chains fell off...."

                      Negro Spiritual

INTRODUCTION

The present exposition was inspired by the author's belief that though nearly everyone concerned with American slavery has had a say, it remains still true that in the present age we have often forgotten the testimony of its victims. The language and style of the times have changed. A testimony of slavery written by an ex-slave is admittedly vivid to us moderns. But often the victim's insights are obscured, if not altogether lost, without an historical perspective.

Slavery had articulate and knowledgeable witnesses who were victims of human bondage. And William Wells Brown, because of his prolific writings, was among the few most significant of these observers. So the focus of my historical commentary has followed his career as an abolitionist writer while attempting to convey the horror of his life as a slave. Slavery made him propagandist of anti-slavery tracts, novels and plays; slavery made him a champion of black history. From slavery to freedom he was throughout his life enslaved to the cause of universal freedom and equality.

The abolitionist Brown grappled first with the paradox of slavery in a democracy. After Emancipation he confronted the paradox of racism in a republic under a color-blind Constitution protecting its citizens from racial persecution. His observations on racism should be of special interest to us today, since that evil remains with us still. He was a great publicist. His gifts were a florid imagination and a fine logical instinct for venting what were slavery's personal contradictions. He had prodigious energy, hope and courage. I hope my efforts here bring his work to a wider, contemporary audience.

William Wells Brown (1813-1884) spent the first twenty years of his life in slavery. The next nine years of his life were spent in relative obscurity as a fugitive. He gained national prominence in the 1840s as a crusader against the peculiar institutions of slavery. His contributions to the abolitionist movement were highly regarded by such notables as William Lloyd Garrison and Wendell Phillips.

Brown has been called the first black American historian and novelist. In spite of the fact that he published more than a dozen books and pamphlets, he has generally been ignored by the historians of American literature. Up until this point, the American reform movement has accorded Brown only limited recognition.

In considering Brown's writings I have used the corpus of his published works, especially The Narrative of William Wells Brown, a Fugitive Slave, 1847, a small volume of one hundred and ten pages which became the best seller among slave narratives published before the Civil War. In 1853, he published Clotel, or the President's Daughter, a novel, which exposes the evils and horrors of human bondage.

Before the end of the Civil War, Brown set about rescuing black history from the limbo to which the pro-slavery sentiment had relegated it. He sought to accomplish this task in one of his best historical works, entitled The Black Man, His Antecedents, His Genius, and His Achievements, 1863. Brown devotes most of his discussion combating the charges of inherent Negro inferiority, because he believed that as long as the doctrine of racial inferiority prevailed, the abolitionists' cause would remain at a decided disadvantage.

In Brown's fictive and dramatic works, he progressed from simply showing the horror of slavery by describing it, to giving an analysis of the racial situation. Brown, in contrast to many other abolitionists, maintained that the struggle for equality would be long and tedious, because the emancipation freed the slave but ignored the problem of Negro equality. Thus, in the post war years, Brown continued to offer analysis and understanding to a complex phenomenon in American history and American Christianity.

MY CHAINS FELL OFF

CHAPTER I

SANDFORD'S LOT

The ancestry of William Wells Brown, like that of most blacks born in American slavery, has been almost lost to history. Brown, in his narrative, stated that his mother was a slave by the name of Elizabeth, but he lacked information about her parents. Still, it was from his mother that he learned of his father, a wealthy, white man named George Higgins who came from Kentucky.

Since Brown's mother was a field hand, it is safe to guess that he was born in the rural area near Lexington rather than in the city. This line of reasoning is supported by Brown's daughter Josephine, who wrote <u>Biography of an American Bondman</u>. Brown's master usually recorded the dates of birth of his slaves, although there appears not to be any record of Brown's birth in that book. This omission is not surprising, because slaveholders often found it advantageous to keep slaves ignorant of their ages. One presumes that masters did not want their slaves to learn how to count, since the possession of an arithmetic, no matter how rudimentary, enables one to calculate odds and predict. But there was the more obvious financial reason. A notorious slave trader, James Walker, sold old slaves for higher prices by having their grey hairs dyed, plucked out, or shaved off and then falsifying their ages. If the slave did not know his age, the seller could conceal it without much fear of embarrassment. To keep the slave ignorant of his age, although he might be an old man, gave a sinister meaning to the white master's hailing any black male as "boy" and any black female as "girl," whether slave or free. Frederick Douglass wrote in 1845: "I was not allowed to make any inquiries of my master concerning age. He deemed all such inquiries on the part of a slave improper and impertinent, and evidence of a restless spirit." Brown gives no specific date of birth anywhere in his narrative. The only reference to his age is the following sentence: "The slave is brought up to look upon every white man as an enemy to him and his race; and twenty-one years in slavery had taught me that there were traitors even among colored people." He was referring to the situation in which he found himself in January of 1834, a few days after he had escaped from slavery. Based on the number of years that he was a slave, Brown must have been born in 1813. His childhood was such as to provide him with

1

the kind of educational tools as to make this estimate almost a certainty.

At the time of Brown's birth, his mother was a slave on a plantation near Lexington, Kentucky belonging to Dr. John Young, half-brother to Brown's father. Young was a physician and made the slave child assist him in his profession. Brown's elevated slave calling as a child stemmed not so much from consanguinity as from his unique function in the Young household. As it is generally known, the condition of the house slaves differed from that of those who worked in the field. The most important difference was that "house niggers" seldom did arduous physical labor all the time. And their general living conditions were milder than the beastly pens of "field niggers." The Youngs had no children of their own. But while Brown was still a boy, his master and mistress adopted a relative's child. Brown's narrative is not reliable as to the origins of the child, for in one place the infant is identified as William Moore and in another described as the son of Young's brother Benjamin.

At any rate the white youth's name was William as so was Brown's. When the adopted boy became old enough to need a playmate and guardian, Brown's mistress organized an exacting contest among the slave children. Brown, to the elation of his mother, was the winner and so he "bade farewell to the log hut and dirt floor, and started toward the 'Big House.'" But Brown's new role as house servant had an unexpected and unpleasant consequence for his sensitive psyche. Two "Williams" in one house were deemed confusing especially since both children were related to Dr. Young. So the Youngs resolved the problem by changing the name of William the slave to Sandford.

Years later Brown would refer to this power of the slavemaster to change the slave's name as a particularly degrading aspect of slavery. For a new master might often change a slave's name and this indicated that the slave had absolutely no rights which a white person was bound to respect. Brown railed against this mortification of the slave's soul some thirty years before Chief Justice Taney condemned the slave to just such an absence of rights.

In 1816 Young moved from Kentucky to Missouri. He took about forty of his slaves with him, including Brown, his mother, sister and two brothers. Brown's other three brothers remained in service on Young's farm in Kentucky. His new farm was located on the Missouri River and his principal products were tobacco and hemp.

Four years later Young became a member of the lower house of the General Assembly of Missouri. Because of his political involvement, he left the management of his farm to his overseer, Cook, who summoned his slaves to work at 4:30 a.m. A slave who was late to work received ten lashes from the whip. Brown describes the whip as being about three feet long, with the butt-end filled with lead, the last, six or seven feet in length, made of rawhide, with platted wire on the end of it. One of Brown's earliest recollections of the cruelty of slavery was when his mother was severely disciplined for being a few minutes late for work. "I could hear every crack of the whip, and every groan and cry of my poor mother," he writes. "I remained at the door, not daring to venture any further." Even had Brown been old enough to defend his mother, it would have been futile for her and surely suicidal for him to intervene. To do so would have brought down the wrath of the slaveholder upon him for daring to raise his hand against a white man.

The slave quarters of Brown's youth were cabins which were generally without windows or floors, and furnished with crude benches, chairs, and tables, and only hard, dirty bunks for beds. The field slaves worked from dawn until night, even in inclement weather. The slaves ate what was cooked for them by a slave who kept the quarters kitchen. Usually the food cooked in the kitchen did not smell, look, nor taste good enough to stimulate one's appetite. Nevertheless, none of the food was wasted, because seldom did everyone get enough to eat. The slaves' clothes were made of coarse cloth, and their shoes were rough and ill-fitting--if they had shoes at all. Slaves were severely beaten at the slightest indication that they wanted to assert any semblance of independence. Brown gave a moving account of what happened to a slave who sought to affirm his humanity in his recollection of the slave Randall.

Strong and well-proportioned, Randall was admired for his strength. But he often bragged defiantly that no white man should ever whip him, "that he would die first." Inevitably this defiance ran afoul of the white overseer Cook. The slave was clubbed into submission, lashed to ribbons and had brine washed into his wounds.

Randall was then compelled to work with a ball and chain tied to his leg. All this had the effect of breaking the man's spirit. Randall's demise is a gripping example of the slave's life under constant terror. The "cliometric" school of historians (see Time on the Cross by Robert W. Fogel and Stanley Engerman, volumes 1 & 2, 1974, Little, Brown, Boston) have argued that slavery was not a physically abusive process as measured by the average daily number of whippings a slave received. But clearly it is of no consequence whether Randall was whipped only once a day or once a week. His reduction to a suppliant minion was caused by one brutal experience and the potential threat of another should he attempt to assert his human dignity. No measure of the number of whippings, their severity or frequency, can indicate the harshness of the slave's lot under constant terror. A whipping merely reinforced the reality of such terror in the slave's consciousness. The slave was forced to behave as though he lived in constant fear of his master (often by stereotypical shuffling and agitated physical movements in the master's presence). A slave who failed to mimic a terrified hysteric did so at the risk of appearing not to have been "broken" and being labeled as "uppity." The slave had to guard against letting his natural instinct for human dignity manifest itself.

Brown's fair complexion burdened him with the peculiar frustration of a marginal man. Because he resembled his paternal relatives, visitors at the Young home sometimes not only failed to recognize him as a slave, but even assumed that he was a member of the family. When Mrs. Young discovered that visitors made such mistakes, she became vexed and would scorn and whip Brown. He was treated as though he was the cause rather than an incidental effect of his father's licentiousness. This was an occasion for the master's wife to be embarrassed, particularly when some remote and unknowing visitor might see Brown and declare him the "doctor's son."

Brown's Caucasian ancestry and European features made other slaves resent and perhaps envy him. Aware of this racialized consciousness Brown attempted to describe its psychology for the first time in literature. A color consciousness was uniquely created by a color obsession; and Brown learned that the obsession manifested itself in unique behavioral values. In Brown's words:

> The nearer a slave approaches an Anglo-Saxon
> in complexion, the more he is abused by both
> owner and fellow-slaves. The owner flogs him
> to keep him "in his place," and the slaves
> hate him on account of his being whiter than
> themselves. Thus, the complexion of the slave
> becomes a crime, and he made to curse his
> father for the Anglo-Saxon blood that courses
> through his veins. (1)

No doubt the alien African slave when first brought to American shores (like the Indians who greeted the first Europeans) had the aracial values of Shakespeare's Othellian world. Appearance of physical difference had virtually no socially important values; nationality, in the sense of language, religion and polity, was the determining value in social perception among people of different races. But the rapid anglocization of the tribal African almost required that racial difference become the basis for defining a slave; as the African became less of a Mandinke and more of a black-Christian-Scotch-Irish-American planter, race no longer reflected his subjugation but had to define it. Otherwise whites lost a safety net and could replace their black slaves, by having lost the protection of a white skin.

In 1827 Young moved to St. Louis and purchased a farm four miles from the city. While he practiced medicine, he left his farm under the supervision of Friend Haskel, a Yankee from New England. The slave community believed the northerners who migrated south to become slaveholders or overseers were notoriously ruthless and cruel. Certainly Haskel's behavior towards slaves strengthened the belief. No doubt Brown realized that white attitudes towards Negroes were not materially much different in either region. The concentration of Negroes and interracial contact, on the other hand, might mean the difference between white susceptibility to anti-slavery sentiment and white hostility, or indifference. When white factory workers in the north lived not much easier than many plantation slaves, it was difficult to light the fire of moral indignation in whites over slavery. For Brown it was important to make whites in the north not want to be slaveholders, nor to sympathize with white slavers. The absence of a large black population gave the abolitionist a fertile ground to accomplish this attitude in the popular northern press. Given uniform prejudice in the white population, the north might never have gone to war simply to free the southern slaves. But the abolitionists made the north realize its regional interest in not seeing the peculiar institution spread. It was the abolitionist, moreover, who in the darkest hour of the Civil War made the north realize that freeing the slaves could wreck the Confederate economy. With a motive similar to that of the north, in one of history's sublime lessons in human irony, the Confederacy itself proclaimed an Emancipation Proclamation. Just two weeks before the Confederacy surrendered, any slave who joined the Confederate Army was declared a free man. White northerners, who might have been like Haskell (at least in racial attitudes) then had an urgent need to free southern blacks. Then, too, it was only the southern black slaves that the north's Emancipation Proclamation initially freed. Abolitionist sentiment was needed to quickly amend the oversight to black slaves in the rest of the country.

Region then made little difference in white attitudes towards blacks. A northerner like Haskell had no reason not to drive black slaves as hard as a white southerner. Fortunately for Brown and his mother they were hired out rather than subjected to the excesses of transient overseers.

Brown's principal place of residence during his last six years of slavery was St. Louis. It was not unusual for slave owners to hire their slaves out for additional income. On one such occasion, the notorious slave trader, James Walker, paid Young nine hundred dollars for Brown's service for one year. Brown was an excellent worker and his service yielded high prices for his owner. Young frequently hired him out. During the St. Louis years Brown was the private property of only three slaveholders, but he worked during the period for at least ten different persons--seven in addition to his three owners. The frequent change in employers and varied positions proved helpful in acquainting him with the many facets of the institution of slavery. Years later when he became an anti-slavery agent, he could speak against slavery from a broad and knowledgeable background.

Initially Brown and his mother were hired out to Major Freeland, whom Brown described as a "horse-racer, cockfighter, gambler, and withal an inveterate drunkard whose fits of anger would cause him to throw chairs at his servants and put them in the smokehouse."

Brown was in Freeland's service only a short time before he found it necessary to report to his owner the bad treatment he was receiving, but his report won him no sympathy as long as the owner compensated for the slave's work. After tolerating Freeland's cruelty for five or six months, he ran away to the woods near St. Louis. His flight was futile and brief. Within a few days, he was captured by two slave catchers with the aid of bloodhounds. He was returned to Freeland. With the assistance of his son, Freeland whipped Brown severely and then shut him up in a smokehouse, had a fire made of tobacco stem near him, and left him to be smoked until he almost suffocated. This practice, called "Virginia Play," was intended to break Brown's spirit. And in a slave conditioned to such brutality this might have been the effect, but Brown's slave background made him only react against this treatment, not respond to it.

From the service of Freeland Brown was employed in the steward's department of the steamboat Missouri, which plied between St. Louis and Galena, Illinois. The employment lasted only a few months. Brown was then hired as one of twenty-one servants at the Missouri Hotel in St. Louis. The innkeeper was John Colburn, a northerner. While working for Colburn, Brown learned something about the intricacies of slavery and romance. One of the hired slaves at the Missouri Hotel was Patsey, who was in love with John, the property of Major William Christy, one of the prominent citizens of St. Louis County. Because of his own amorous interest in Patsey, Colburn forbade her to bestow any attention upon John. Finding that she had disobeyed him by letting John walk home with her one evening, Colburn decided to whip John, but could not catch him. Vengeance, nevertheless, must still be his; so he tied Patsey up "and whipped her until several of the boarders came out and begged him to desist." Slavery was a system of frustrated and aborted controls; excessive cruelty would be opposed by even a white southern public conscience. Abolitionist Brown would have a good basis for continuing his appeals to white conscience in his portrayal of slavery's excesses.

In the early part of 1830, Brown was hired as a handy boy in the printing office of Reverend Elijah P. Lovejoy, editor and publisher of the St. Louis Times. Brown worked for Lovejoy over a period of about six months. Writing in his narrative, he described Lovejoy as "a good man and decidedly the best master that I had ever had. I am chiefly indebted to him, and to my employment in the printing office, for what little learning I obtained while in slavery." Unfortunately, this opportunity would only whet his appetite for learning, since it was brutally interrupted after a brief time. Although Brown worked for Lovejoy, his employer could not protect the slave in conflict with a white. Brown was attacked by a white gang of youths and tried to defend himself. His escape resulted in an alleged injury to one of the youths. The boy's father came to Lovejoy's office to punish Brown who then had to flee. When the matter was settled Brown's coveted job belonged to someone else. Everywhere there was uncertainty and instability. Under slavery, merit could not rise and the progress of the mind was retarded. Innovation in the arts and sciences was dangerous to the prevailing social order. The slaveocracy might copy and adapt to invention from free societies but the slave states were unable to pursue independent lines of technical development. And white society was immobilized by its repression of the slaves.

When Brown recovered from injuries suffered in the Lovejoy incident, he was hired to the steward's department of the steamboat <u>Enterprise</u>, which was engaged in the river trade from St. Louis northward. He was exposed to the environment of freedom on the northern voyages of the steamboat. He wrote:

> In passing from place to place, and seeing new faces every day, and knowing that they could go where they pleased, I soon became unhappy, and several times thought of leaving the boat at some landing place, and trying to make my escape to Canada, which I had heard much about as a place where the slave might live, be free, and be protected. (2)

It was a brief glimpse of the possible. Presently Brown was returned to his master's plantation and put to work under Haskell. The overseer disregarded the fact that Brown was not accustomed to field work; he demanded as much work from him as he did from the regular field hands, and flogged him when he failed to do it.

Young returned to reside on the plantation and he immediately restored Brown to his position as house servant. He was made part-time assistant to the physician, his principal duties being to prepare medicines, administer to ailing slaves, and run errands. This experience led to lifelong interest in the medical profession. In middle age, long since a freeman, he formally studied medicine and became a practicing physician. Slavery never dimmed his interest but also never permitted him to realize his talents.

CHAPTER II

A STRANGE AND CRUEL DEMOCRACY

A religious sensibility was natural to the slave but the opportunities for worship and practice were denied the slaves until the institution became well established. Young kept most of his slaves so busy working for him from dawn to night that they had time to do little or nothing for themselves. The only free time they had was on Sunday; and this day they generally spent gardening, hunting, fishing, washing and mending their clothes, or making brooms and baskets for sale. When Young got religion, he stopped all secular activities on Sunday. He compelled the slaves to attend Sabbath meetings. Going still further, he got other slaveholders to co-operate with him in hiring a preacher for the slaves. He remembered the Sabbath Day, to keep it holy, but the fullness of spirit for the master frequently ended in empty stomachs for the slaves.

Brown realized that the slaveholders were much less interested in saving the souls of their slaves than in having religion bestowed upon them as a means of making them good slaves. He observed that his slave master's religion taught that God had made them to be slaves, and that they could serve their heavenly master best by being satisfied with their status and being subservient and faithful in all things to their earthly master. Insofar as the slavemaster was concerned, wrote Brown:

> Their religious teaching consists in teaching the slave that he must never strike a white man; that God made him for a slave; and that, when whipped, he must not find fault--for the Bible says, 'He that knoweth his master's will and doeth it not, shall be beaten with many stripes!' and slaveholders find such religion very profitable. (3)

Some of the most ruthless slaveholders of Brown's experience were churchmen. Brown tells of a time when he was returning from church, and passed the house of a slaveholder who, chasing a female slave in his yard, stumbled and fractured his own leg. After he apprehended the slave, he whipped her nearly to death. Brown contended that she was beaten beyond recognition, but he was careful to point out in his narrative that after the slaveholder committed the merciless act, "He did not lose respect among his fellow churchmen for doing so."

Brown was convinced that no segment of society, whether religious or political, could divorce itself from the evil of slavery. As to religion, Brown wrote: "The slaves regarded the religious profession of the whites around us as a farce...and (preachers) ...as mere hypocrites." (4) But the fact remained that through religion, now encouraged by the slavemasters, the slave came to possess a measure of the ethical contradictions of slavery. From then on it no longer mattered that slaves were forbidden to learn to count and read. A religious devotion provided more knowledge, defiance and cunning than any rote acquisition of literacy.

In 1832 Young hired Brown for one year to James Walker, the passenger Brown had known on the <u>Enterprise</u>. Walker was an unrelenting slave trader. Brown said that Young received nine hundred dollars from Walker for Brown's services. This price was exceptionally high for slave men in Missouri. Walker paid the high price for Brown possibly because he was impressed with his work when they had first met on the <u>Enterprise</u>. Walker felt that Brown would make a good custodian of slaves and had tried to purchase him earlier. Brown attributes Young's refusal to their kinship.

Brown became Walker's caretaker. They set out for St. Louis on a Mississippi River steamboat with a miscellaneous group of between fifty and seventy-five slaves for the markets in the Mississippi delta. After disposing of the slaves, they returned to St. Louis and made preparation for another cargo of slaves. Although Brown was depressed with his slave trading role, he was compelled to work for Walker the term of his lease.

Before the slaves were exhibited for sale, they were dressed and cleaned up. Then they were driven into the slave pen. To make them appear happy, they were trained to dance, play cards and sing. It was Brown's job to make them appear happy and cheerful. Brown lamented, "I have set them to dancing when their cheeks were wet with tears."

Immediately upon their return to St. Louis, they went on another slave-buying expedition. At the completion of the purchase of slaves, the blacks were herded like cattle and set on a forced walk of twenty miles to Walker's farm in St. Louis. A black woman was purchased who had a baby four or five months old. On their way to the farm, the baby was crying. The crying annoyed Walker and he took the baby from his mother and gave the baby to a family he had stayed with the night before.

On a delivery to Vicksburg, Brown accidentally spilled something on one of Walker's customers. Brown was sent with a note to get a whipping from the local jailer. On the way Brown learned of his fate. He deceived an unwary freedman to take the note and deliver it. Later Brown regretted this mean deception, observing that slavery "makes its victims lying and mean." Indeed the slave's morality was of the most self-interested kind. Right and wrong were warped by the desperate struggle to avoid persecution and pain. Slaves oppressed other slaves. The most powerful reigned and deception was a survival technique of those who were most cunning.

When he had completed his turn of service with Walker, "the longest year I ever lived," Brown returned to St. Louis. His position as overseer and caretaker of his fellow slaves had horrified him but undoubtedly he had acquired important knowledge of the powers and controls of the slavemasters.

That year Young decided to sell Brown but would not allow the slave to make arrangements to buy his own freedom. This came as a cruel blow. In the past, whenever he considered running away, he dismissed the notion since he would have had to abandon his mother. And now, though his mother urged him to escape, he refused unless she agreed to accompany him.

Brown's deep and unending affection and devotion for his mother is indicative of the importance he placed upon family. Now that he had persuaded her to join him in his escape, they set out that night in search of freedom in Canada. They successfully escaped across the Mississippi River into Illinois. They hid by day and traveled by night. But the tenth day, exhausted by inclement weather and hunger, their hope of freedom was shattered. Bounty hunters overtook them and the slaves were apprehended.

It had taken Brown and his mother eleven days to travel about one hundred and fifty miles. In their quest for freedom they had committed an unpardonable sin. Punishment was inevitable. A captured runaway was usually sold and transported to the deep south. When Brown and his mother were relased from jail, however, they had to appear before Young. His owner asked where Brown had been. Brown replied: "I told (him)

I had acted according to his orders. He had told me to look for a master, and I had been looking for one." Brown had become the plaintiff: "I told him that as I had served him faithfully, and had been the means of putting a number of hundreds of dollars into his pocket, I thought I had a right to my liberty."

Young had vowed never to sell Brown to supply the New Orleans market. He now honored this promise by sending the slave to work in his field as punishment instead. Young would not send his slave to the hard overseers in the deep south, but he had Brown worked especially hard and saw that the slave was whipped for the least error. Brown was kept under a watchful eye by day and locked up at night. After a few weeks of this regime, Brown was sold to a merchant tailor for five hundred dollars. Brown's new owner was named Willis.

Brown's mother remained in prison. Through the slave "grapevine" he learned that his mother was being sold to a slaveholder in New Orleans. As she was leaving, Brown went to bid her farewell. He felt especially sad because he considered himself responsible for her fate. But she consoled him by assuring him that he had done his duty.

While Brown was grieving with his mother, one of the bounty hunters kicked Brown and ordered him to leave the steamboat. He stayed on the wharf and watched the steamboat carry his mother away from him forever. He recorded the scene in heart-rending prose: "As I left her, she gave one shriek, saying, 'God be with you!' It was the last time that I saw her, and the last word I heard her utter. I walked on shore. The bell was tolling, the boat was about to start. I stood with a heavy heart, waiting to see her leave." Of all his experiences under slavery this must have caused Brown the most remorse.

Although Brown was treated better by Willis than by Young the distinction was no longer important. Slavery was bad at its best; freedom was good at its worst. He recalled his mother's words: "You have even said that you would not die a slave; that you would be a freeman. Now try to get your liberty!" He began to dream and plot for his liberty.

In the fall of 1833 Willis sold Brown to a St. Louis commission merchant and steamboat owner, Enoch Price. According to Brown, Price paid seven hundred dollars for him. Brown was to serve as a coachman. Mrs. Price was status-conscious and she wanted her slaves to make a good appearance. Brown thus wore new clothes and drove the fanciest coach. Mrs. Price knew that family ties inhibited the slaves' desire to escape. So she tried to facilitate slave marriages.

Brown was encouraged to marry a slave girl named Maria. Brown was already in love with another slave named Eliza, however, and the object of his affection had to be purchased from another master. Brown, in spite of his affection, knew that slave marriages were unrecognized by law and the vows an exercise in absurdity. Slave families were subject to sudden and regular separation. Any slave who believed that his family could be nourished and preserved as a unit was only creating future grief. And it would not be long in coming.

Most slaves did not have Brown's formal education, if such it could be called, but they were well educated in the "peculiar customs" of slavery. They understood the slavemaster's motives in encouraging slave marriages. One may only speculate as to how much of this slave cynicism towards marriage survives in the unrecorded folk culture of black people today. Brown had seen the partners in a new marriage separated by their master and compelled to marry new partners. Brown in fact was determined not to get married until he was free. He thus promised to marry Eliza so as to remove the pressure from Mrs. Price as well as not to upset the girl. But he never declared a day.

A few weeks after Price purchased Brown the household, including slaves, visited New Orleans. While there Price decided to continue his journey by the same steamer up to Cincinnati. Price was apprehensive about taking Brown into a free state but Brown dissembled and lied that at last he and Eliza were married. The Price household arrived in Cincinnati so confident of Brown's loyalty that the slaves were not required to unload the baggage until the next morning. It was December 31, 1833; no doubt everyone was in a festive New Year's spirit.

CHAPTER III

WILLIAM WELLS

January 1, 1834, was not only the beginning of a new year. It was the day Brown walked hurriedly through the crowded city, not stopping until he reached a marshy woodland, in his second bid for freedom. The day was cold. But Brown hid in the woods until night. Then, knowing no guide but the North Star, he made his way in the direction of Canada.

On the fourth day of his flight, Brown was in the western part of Ohio. He had no food, he was suffering from exposure to the frigid weather, and he lacked clothing as well. Brown decided to forage for food rather than try to buy or beg because he was afraid to be seen by anyone. He did not want to take the risk of being identified as a fugitive and recaptured. He was yet sustained by these thoughts:

> When I thought of slavery, with its democratic whips, its republican chains, its evangelical bloodhounds, and its religious slaveholders--when I thought of all this paraphernalia of American democracy and religion behind me, and the prospect of liberty before me, I was encouraged to press forward, my heart was strengthened, and I forgot that I was tired or hungry. (5)

Brown was caught on the fifth or sixth day in a freezing rain. He traveled on at night until he became so chilled and benumbed that he had to take shelter in a barn. There he had to walk about to keep from freezing. "Nothing but the providence of God," he remembered, "and that old barn saved me from death." He caught a terrible cold and his feet were so badly frost-bitten that it was painful for him to walk. As Brown's will for freedom grew stronger, his body grew weaker. He concealed himself behind logs and bushes along the roadside until he could get some help.

He watched the road to sight a sympathetic face. Finally he approached an old man on foot. The man's dress and demeanor indicated that he was not hostile to blacks. The man asked Brown if he was a fugitive slave and upon Brown's assent offered to transport the slave to a less hostile neighborhood. Brown had found a Quaker and was escorted under a covered wagon to the man's house.

At first the slave was reluctant to enter the man's house, but the man's wife convinced the slave of their sincerity. They doctored him until he regained his strength.

In spite of his friendly treatment, Brown felt uncomfortable; the transition from slave to freeman was too abrupt. He felt as though he was in a dream.

Brown's benefactor was like any number of Quakers of the day. The Friends tended to treat slaves as human beings. When the Quaker asked Brown his full name, the fugitive replied that it was only William. "Well," said his white comrade, "thee must have another name. Since thee has got out of slavery, thee has become a man, and men always have two names." Since this Quaker was the first man to extend a hand of friendship to him, Brown wanted to be named for his friend. But he was not yet willing to throw away the name William. Until he escaped from slavery William was still Sandford. But now his Quaker friend, who was called William Wells, said, "I will call thee William Wells Brown."

Brown was now a new man with a new name, new clothes, new shoes, and a new determination to reach Canada. Within four days, he traveled half of the distance from central Ohio to Cleveland, but by this time he was out of food. He stopped one day at a public house, and while stopping, he heard some people talking about a fugitive slave. He feared he would be identified and recaptured.

Taking refuge in wooded areas by day he made his journey mainly by night. He had been without food for two days before he went to a farm house to beg for food. After an initial amount of hesitation the couple there provided him with food, a few cents and directions to another sympathetic house. In three days he was in Cleveland, Ohio. It was the middle of winter. There was ice on Lake Erie; no steamboats were running. In order to get to Canada, it was necessary to go by land through Buffalo or Detroit. The cold prohibited travel by foot and lack of money made it too costly to travel by stagecoach. Brown decided to remain in Cleveland until the winter ended and navigation across the lake resumed.

Freedom without food, housing and a job was a precarious existence. He accepted employment as a choreman for a family and he was compensated with room and board. Afterwards he worked as a waiter; and in the spring he worked on a steamer on Lake Erie.

Brown felt a greater sense of security travelling and working on the steamboat than he felt on land. This job gave him the opportunity to learn about free places in the U.S. and Canada. It was also a lucrative job. But more importantly Brown's position enabled him to begin carrying fugitive slaves to Canada by way of Detroit and Buffalo. Thus he became an abolitionist long before he joined the Anti-Slavery Society.

In his new freedom Brown subscribed to the <u>Liberator</u>, edited by William Lloyd Garrison; he also read the "Genius of Universal Emancipation," published by Benjamin Lundy. But it would be ten years later before Brown became a formal agent of the Western New York Anti-Slavery Society.

CHAPTER IV

FREEDOM

Brown's primary efforts and interest in writing, however genuine, were secondary to goals--that is, he used his writing to accomplish specific ends. In his historical writings he is concerned to demonstrate the inherent error in the assumption that blacks are by nature inferior in ability and intelligence. The author's biographical presentation of his own history and his consideration of black history demonstrate occasions and personalities which illustrate both the prejudice he is attacking and the validity of his own position.

In 1855 William Wells Brown published an account and evaluation of his years abroad. The American Fugitive in Europe, which was essentially an American edition of Three Years in Europe, published in London in 1852. The two books provided a historical account of Brown's 1849 trip to Europe, on which he was sent as a delegate to the Paris Peace Congress. While in Europe, he visited France and the British Isles, travelling twenty-five thousand miles to lecture on American Slavery and to plead the cause of abolition.

After ten days of travel from Boston on the Canada, he arrived at Liverpool. The custom officers who inspected Brown's luggage found an iron collar that had been worn by a female slave on the banks of the Mississippi. When the ex-slave was questioned about the instrument, Brown described it as the "democratic instrument of torture." His fellow white American passengers were visibly displeased with Brown's explanation.

On the voyage to Europe, one of his fellow passengers made racial slurs about Brown's presence on the ship. He said, "That Nigger had better be on his master's farm," and "what could the American Peace Society be thinking about to send a black man as a delegate to Paris."

Brown contrasts the difference between race relationships in his native land and Britain. He wrote:

> The prejudice which I have experienced on all and every occasion in the United States, and to some extent on board the Canada, vanished as soon as I set foot on the soil of Britain. In America, I had been bought and sold as a slave in the southern states.

> I had been treated as one born to occupy
> an inferior position--in steamers, compelled
> to take my fare on the deck; in hotels, to
> take my meals in the kitchen; in coaches,
> to ride on the outside; in railways, to ride
> in the 'Negro-car,' and in churches, to sit
> in the 'Negro pew.' But no sooner was I
> on British soil, than I was recognized as a
> man, and an equal. (6)

Brown was highly visible at the Peace Congress; he was introduced to the eminent Victor Hugo. His fellow Americans who had been horrified with having to ride on the Canada with him, now requested him to introduce them to the celebrity attending the conference, but he declined to introduce his "pro-slavery Americans" to this distinguished man. Brown wrote:

> The man who would not have been seen walking
> with me in the streets of New York, and who
> would not have shaken hands with me with a
> pair of tongs while on the passage from the
> United States, could come with hat in hand
> in Paris, and say, "I was your fellow passen-
> ger." (7)

Brown expressed mixed emotions in his evaluation of the Peace Conference; on the one hand, it was glorious and on the other it was "nice child play." By consenting to restrict their discussion of topics, the congress was gagged before it got started. Brown said, "They put the padlocks upon their own mouths, and handed the key to the government."

At the close of the Peace Congress, M. Alexis de Tocqueville, the French foreign Minister, invited Brown to his home. "In America, I would not have been at such a gathering, unless as a servant," said Brown. At the gathering, Brown conversed with Pierre Jean de Baranger, "the people's poet" of France. The poet expressed strong opposition to slavery and questioned how America reconciled slavery with her professed love of freedom.

When Brown left France, he went to Britain where he spent the majority of his time while abroad. From his arrival he was identified with the cause of abolition. This initial visit was with a Mr. George Thompson, a distinguished British abolitionist to whom William Lloyd Garrison had written an introductory letter.

Brown began his crusade for freedom on the British soil in Newcastle. In his speech at Newcastle, Brown contrasts the lot of slaves to that of the labouring class in Britain. He said:

> Whatever may be the disadvantage that the British peasant labours under, he is free; and if he is not satisfied with his employer he can make choice of another. He also has the right to educate his children. The American slave has no right, no right to protect his wife, his child, or his own person. He is nothing more than a living tool.

Brown maintained that a slave has no rights in court, except the mere will of his owner. He is deprived of worship and religious training. Brown exhorted the British people to judge America on her practices rather than her noble principles.

Whatever English folk thought of America, they received Brown warmly. James Montgomery, the British poet, expressed amazement that American slaveholders could maintain membership in the church. In Leeds, Brown had the good fortune of meeting with Wilson Armistead, Esq., the well known author of "A Tribute for the Negro," a refutation of the charge of inherent Negro inferiority. Brown commended Armistead for his labour toward the emancipation of American slaves.

On New Year's Day, 1851, Brown visited Edinburgh with William Craft who was also a fugitive slave. They were guests of the Edinburgh Ladies' Emancipation Society. Craft gave a history of his escape from Macon, Georgia, and powerfully impressed the audience. Brown said he wished Craft's ex-slaveholders Hughes and Knight could have been present and heard the thundering applause their ex-slave received.

Brown visited Oxford and Cambridge Universities, and spoke with Alexander Crummel, who was studying at Cambridge. Proud of blacks matriculating at these great universities, Brown gave a lecture of encouragement to Crummel by pointing to Toussaint who laboured in the sugar field with a spelling book in his pocket, and emerged as a great emancipator and statesman. Brown reminded Crummel that "it is not always those who have the best advantages, or the greatest talents, that eventually succeed in their undertakings, but it is those who strive to remove all obstacles to success." (8)

In August of 1851, a number of fugitives from America assembled with Brown at the Hall of Commerce in the city of London, to lay their wrongs before the British nation, and at the same time to give thanks to the God of Freedom for liberation of the West Indies brethren, on August 1, 1834. The American fugitives were accompanied by George Thompson, Esq.; Reverend Jabez Burns, D. D.; Reverend John Stevenson, M.A.; William Farmer, Esq.; and R. Smith, Esq., who were some of the oldest and most devoted Englishmen to the abolitionise cause.

Brown took the position at the meeting that the abolition of slavery in the West Indies was a step in the right direction, and one that would eventually lead to abolition in America. He reported that it was often said by Americans that England was responsible for the advent of slavery in the U.S. They charged England with introducing slavery to America. Brown argued that, if that were the case, they must come to the conclusion that, as England abolished slavery in the West Indies, she would have done the same for the American States if she had had the power to do it. England had set the noble example.

The fugitive slave law, argued Brown, was sufficient proof that the northern states were in sympathy with the slaveholders in the south. The fugitive was afforded no protection, no opportunity of proving his right to be free. The fugitive slave law converted the whole population of the free states into a band of slave catchers.

Brown wrote an appeal that was adopted at the close of the meeting. The appeal pointed to the part that declaration of independence declared "that all men are created equal," yet one-sixth of the inhabitants of the great Republic were slaves.

The appeal argued that the passage of the inhuman Fugitive Slave Law would not have been possible without the support of the free states. Moreover, the passage of the fugitive bill compelled many free blacks to seek refuge in the British possessions in North America.

The abolitionist, Brown, changed his tone after the passage of the Fugitive Slave act from "moral persuasion" to a "new militancy." His new aggressiveness is expressed in an 1854 London lecture, where he cautioned his audience that if the moral struggle for freedom failed, a physical one would be inevitable.

> Already the slaves in chains in the rice
> swamps of Carolina and the cotton fields
> of Mississippi are burning for revenge. (9)

Brown appealed to Britain to use all lawful and peaceful pressure on American slaveholders to restore to blacks their God-given rights. He called upon the British clergymen to exclude pro-slavery ministers from their pulpits and communion. In short, Brown sought to consolidate international public opinion against the institution of human bondage.

In 1863, from Boston, there appeared one of Brown's ablest and best-known works bearing the title: <u>The Black Man: His Antecedents, His Genius, and His Achievements</u>. In the preface, he set forth the two purposes of the work. First he wrote to combat the pro-slavery advocates who argued the "natural inferiority" of the blacks, and their destiny for a servile condition. Secondly, he wrote to inform those adversaries who were ignorant of the character, genius, and intellectual development of individual Negroes.

> If this work shall aid in vindicating the
> Negro's character, and show that he is
> endowed with those intellectual and amiable
> qualities which adorn and dignify human
> nature, it will meet the most sanguine
> hopes of the writer. (10)

Brown sought to achieve his first purpose by means of the initial essay entitled, "The Black Man and His Antecedent." He admitted that after two-and-a-half centuries of Negro enslavement, even the government had affirmed the natural inferiority of the Negro. Brown argued that the Negro had not always been characterized as inferior, and the Anglo-Saxon considered superior, but that on the contrary there were periods in history when Negroes were the leaders of civilization and the Anglo-Saxons were the inferior race. Brown wrote:

> I admit that the condition of my race,
> whether considered in a mental, moral,
> or intellectual point of view, at the
> present time cannot compare favorably
> with the Anglo-Saxon. But it does not
> become the whites to point the finger
> of scorn at the blacks, when they have
> so long been degrading them. The
> Negro has not always been considered

the inferior race. The time was when he
stood at the head of science and literature. (11)

Brown argued that the Negro had attained a high degree of civilization, while the Anglo-Saxons were a
"rude and barbarous people, divided into numerous
tribes, dressed in the skins of wild beasts."

He expressed racial pride in the fact that the black
slaves are descendants of African kings who left monu-
mental inscriptions from Ethiopia to India. No amount
of racial prejudice and hatred could eradicate the at-
tainment of Black Civilization from the pages of history. He realized that civilization, regardless of
color, is not developed in a vacuum, nor racial progress
in isolation from other people. He wrote:

> There is nothing in race or blood, in
> color or features, that imparts sus-
> ceptibility of improvement to one race
> over another. The mind left to itself
> from infancy, without culture, remains
> a blank. Knowledge is not innate. As
> the Greeks and Romans, and Jews drew
> knowledge from the Egyptian three
> thousand years ago, and the Europeans
> received it from the Romans, so must
> the blacks of the land rise in the same
> way. As one man learns from another,
> so nation learns from nation. Civili-
> zation is handed from one people to
> another, its great foundation source
> being God our Father. Already the
> blacks on this continent, though kept
> down under the heel of the white man,
> are fast rising in the scale of intel-
> lectual development, and proving their
> equality with the brotherhood of man. (12)

Brown taxed the New York Herald, Boston Post, Boston Courier and New York Journal of Commerce with mis-
representing the effects of emancipation in the West
Indies. The news media in general had described de-
terioration in the West Indies following the emancipation. Brown argued that "slavery had impoverished the
soil, demoralized the people, and all the islands were
in ruin long before Parliament had passed the act of
emancipation."

He also attempted to refute the assertion that

blacks were incapable of being free by showing some of the accomplishments of free blacks. The free blacks in Maryland and Virginia, who were former slaves or descendants of slaves, had accumulated property and wealth in defiance of prejudiced opinions and laws. The slaveholders believed the mere presence of free prosperous blacks made slaves unhappy and discontent. This was the rationale behind the Southern Rights convention held in Baltimore, Maryland, June 8, 1870, adopting a resolution to drive the free Negroes out of the state.

Brown asserted that the productivity of slaves in the south was one of the foremost obstacles to emancipation. Some slaveholders in the south were economically dependent upon their slaves. Slave owners hired out their slaves and some slave artisans had been known to pay their owners as much as six hundred dollars anually. Slave owners had also been known to have stolen and borrowed money from their industrious and thrifty slaves.

Again, Brown pointed out that when the legislature of South Carolina entertained the idea of expelling the free blacks from the state, a committee appointed to investigate the matter filed the following report: "We find that the free blacks of the state are among our most industrious people; in this city (Charleston) we find that they own over two-and-a-half millions of dollars worth of property; that they pay two thousand seven hundred dollars to the city."

To pro-slavery apologists who argued that "if the slaves are emancipated, we won't receive them upon an equality," Brown admitted that neither society nor the government can make the Negro free by legislation alone. He did not expect the slave of the south to jump into equality, but he should be allowed to jump into liberty: "I have some white neighbors around me in Cambridge," he wrote, "who are not very intellectual; they don't associate with my family; but whenever they shall improve themselves, and bring themselves up by their own intellectual and moral worth, I shall not object to their coming into my society--all things equal." In short, Brown said, "All I demand for the black man is, that the white man shall take their heels off his neck, and let him have a chance to rise by his own efforts."

Brown concluded the initial section of the book by opposing the idea of colonization. He declared that colonization would not be economically feasible. Abolition would improve the economy by making the Negro a consumer. The new black consumer in the south would increase the demand for more manufactured goods in the north. On the other hand, the slave holders would have to go to work and would not have time to "concoct treason against the stars and stripes."

The second part of the book Brown wrote to develop and document the position he had set forth. The section entitled "Black Man, His Genius and His Achievements," offers biographical sketches of fifty-three Negroes who had made outstanding achievements in various literary fields. The list is long and impressive of Blacks who demonstrated ability and achievement in spite of hostility and limited opportunity. The variety is great--from poets to educators. The feature that unites them is a common element of ability, achievement and superiority which distinguishes them in diverse fields and destroys the accusations which Brown was fighting. The biographical presentations support his thesis for abolition and equality.

The cumulative effect is powerful, as Brown meant it to be. Just how powerful is illustrated in recapitulation of selected subjects and details which he treated at greater length, but which contributed to his goal--to liberate the blacks in such fashion as not only to free people of this distinction, but to make possible the development of others like them. Through various individuals, Brown argues that the Black race is as gifted with ability and talent as any other people. He uses personalities and occasions to show that human bondage is both immoral and indefensible. Brown's impressive list of blacks illustrates and illuminates the fine character, courage and stamina of a people who achieved under adverse circumstances.

Brown's tributes to individuals in the black race were meant to refute the pro-slavery sentiment that Negroes by nature are shiftless, childlike, dull-witted and incapable of ascending beyond menial tasks. Brown exhausted every possible resource and opportunity to expose the horrors of slavery and to champion the cause of Negro equality.

CHAPTER V

THE CALL TO BATTLE

Brown's technique was straightforward and effective. In a series of biographical sketches running to almost fifty in number, Brown cites one individual after another whose story illustrates some aspect of the black man's ability and significance, often coupled with the frustration of his opportunity through the cruelty of slavery.

To augment the well-known narratives of Frederick Douglass and his own, Brown cited the autobiography of Henry Bibb. His narrative was a brilliant example of the intellectual accomplishment blacks could achieve. When Harriet Beecher Stowe was preparing to write Uncle Tom's Cabin as a serial for the National Era, she thought of Bibb as one who might give her information regarding the intimate customs of slaves on other plantations. Bibb and his wife settled in Canada, where he became the editor and founder of an abolitionist newspaper called the Voice of Freedom. His wife opened a school to train the fugitives. For Brown the native intelligence and potential of the black was ably illustrated in the account of Bibb's success, once the fugitive was liberated from the inhibitions of slavery.

William C. Nell, like Brown, was one of the first blacks to make a serious attempt at recording the history of their people in America. In his published works he emphasized themes common in the writing of Brown. He was born in 1812, and was a native of Boston, Massachusetts. Nell was mentioned in the abolitionist paper, the Liberator, as "one of the most deserving and exemplary of our colored citizens, amicable and modest in his deportment and intelligent in mind."

Except for a few years which Nell spent in Rochester, New York, where he was for a short time associated with Frederick Douglass in the publication of the North Star, he lived most of his life in Boston working with the abolitionist William Lloyd Garrison. Nell was one of the leaders in petitioning the City of Boston to grant black children the right to attend public school, and in 1855 the black children were permitted to attend the Boston Public Schools.

Brown commemorated the achievements and prowess of Samuel Ringgold Ward, who was born in Maryland in 1817.

When he was approximately three years old, his parents fled with him from Maryland to New York. Ward grew up in what he called "this city of evercrushing Negro hate," received a modest education, and after a few years as a school master became in 1839 a minister of the Congregational Church and an agent of the Anti-Slavery Society. Ward was an effective Anti-Slavery crusader because he disarmed the proslavery sympathizers who charged that the success attributed to Douglass and Brown was due to their white blood. The abolitionists had an answer for such detraction of the Negro in the person of Samuel Ringgold Ward, who, according to Wendell Phillips, was so black that "when he closed his eyes you could not see him."

In addition to making anti-slavery speeches, he served two churches as pastor, one of them being a congregation at South Butler, New York, made up entirely of white parishioners. He wrote:

> The manly courage they showed in calling and sustaining, and honouring as their pastor a black man, in that day, in spite of the too general Negro-hate everywhere, strife (and as professedly pious rife) around them, exposing them as it did to the taunts, jeers, and abuse of too many who wore the cloak of Christianity--entitle them to what they will ever receive, my warmest thanks and kindest love. (13)

Brown labeled Ward as "the black Daniel Webster" because few public speakers, black or white, exercised greater influence on the speakers' platforms.

Brown celebrated the characters of such New Yorkers as Henry Alexander Garnet, James W. C. Pennington, Alexander Crummel and James M'Cune Smith. They all were black clergymen who fought against human bondage and crusaded for Negro equality, and their lives and publications documented Brown's theories.

The Rising Son: or the Antecedents and Advancement of the Colored Race, another of Brown's historical works, published in 1816, took its title from a poem by Elijah W. Smith printed in full on the first page of the volume.

In the first eleven chapters, Brown considers the origin of the Negro race and their antecedents. "The origin of the African race has proved more criticism than any other of the various races of man on the globe. Speculation has exhausted itself in trying to account for the Negro's color, features, and hair, that distinguishes him in such a marked manner from the rest of the human family."

The author attempted to trace the history of the Negro, beginning with Ethiopia through Africa, Latin America, and the United States. The black man can look at his early history with a sense of pride. He is a descendant of the Ethiopians who excelled in government, art, militarism, and hieroglyphics.

Brown argued that the slave trade had been the greatest obstacle to the development of the antecedents to the Negro race. Africans had been enticed to murder, kidnap, burn villages and capture each other for payment in gunpowder and rum, "two of the worst enemies of an ignorant people." Brown contended that the abolition of the slave trade was absolutely necessary for the progress of the race.

Brown devoted chapters twelve through twenty-five to the struggle for freedom in Santo Domingo. He found both instruction and inspiration in the Haitian struggle for freedom.

The slave trade in Santo Domingo, like that in the United States, was precipitated by the need for free labor to till the soil and to work in the mines. As involuntary servitude in the southern states, slavery in Santo Domingo bred amalgamation between masters and slaves. As a consequence, there arose a mulatto population in Santo Domingo that became a thorn in their masters' flesh for freedom and social reform. The planters educated their mulatto sons in France and they returned home inspired to alleviate human bondage in their native land. Names such as Toussaint, Christophe, Dessalines, Petion, Boyer emerged as household names in the struggle for freedom in Santo Domingo.

The numerous details and data in Brown's writings all point to solidifying his anti-slavery ideology. He employed the use of facts and occasions to demonstrate that slavery was unnatural and that abolition would be of mutual benefit to both the slaves and the slaveholders.

In chapters 26-29, Brown gave a brief account of the black abolitionist movement in Jamaica, South America, Cuba and Puerto Rico. In every case Brown pointed to the deep-seated desire for freedom on the part of the slave, and success of the black in achieving this state through contribution of his own ability and resourcefulness.

The political leaders in Jamaica accommodated the British Government by representing the slaves as satisfied to the point that they would not accept freedom if it were offered to them. Samuel Sharp, a deeply religious slave, ended the illusion that slaves were satisfied by leading an insurrection. He persuaded large numbers of slaves that the British Government had set them free but their owners were hiding the fact of their emancipation. The insurrection was suppressed, but his efforts gave new impetus to the abolitionist movement, which culminated in the 1838 Emancipation of the Jamaican people.

Cuba, the stronghold of Spain, in the western world, labored under the disadvantage of slavery for more than 300 years.

In 1830, a talented slave by the mame of Placido wrote poems that were read in society clubs. Placido's literary genius was rewarded with his freedom. He led an attack against the institution of slavery which failed but won the support of abolitionists who continued to agitate for the emancipation of slavery.

In Latin America the abolition of slavery was achieved without a civil war because servitude turned into an economic and social--not color--factor. In the United States the Negro became identified as slave because he was black and consequently remained in a deprived state after emancipation because he would not escape penalty for natural condition even if he managed to evade the legal consequence. Freedom for the Negro in the United States was in a peculiar way different to achieve and that by some was considered undesirable both for the slave and the white man's community.

In Latin America the Negro achieved complete legal equality slowly, through manumission, over the centuries, and after he had acquired some acceptance of his moral personality. On the other hand, in the United States, the Negro was given his freedom suddenly and before the whites credited him with moral status. Miscegenation went on among all classes in the community, and the racial and class mobility was characteristic of southern states unlike slave society in this country. One of the consequences of miscegenation was a social distinction in the colored population which brought a part of the population closer to the master.

In British West Indies it was customary not to put mulattos to work in the sugarcane fields, but rather to keep them as house servants and put them to learn skilled trades. White masters often freed their coloured children and educated them. Even though manumission was rarer in the United States than in the Indies the mulatto got preferential treatment in America

In the British, French, and United States slave systems the law attempted to fix patterns and stratify the social classes and the racial groups. But the law failed. The Haitian rebellion, the Civil War in the United States, and the abolition of slavery in the British West Indies are all results of the same thrust for freedom. The essential likeness of the problem, wherever Brown observed or reported it, implied for him both an inevitable similar outcome, namely abolition, and also--in the interim--an obligation of support and sympathy for abolitionists in America from those of other governments who had already come nearer to the realization of the ultimate goal of true integration.

The largest section of his book, however, Brown devoted to blacks in the United States. The author pointed out that black history in America began simultaneously with the landing of Pilgrims on Plymouth Rock in 1620.

Brown reminded the reader that before the Revolutionary War there was no such distinction as free or slave states. Brown wrote: "When the first census was taken in 1791, the total number of slaves in the north was forty thousand three hundred and seventy; in the southern, six hundred fifty three thousand nine hundred and ten." In short, slavery existed both in the north and south, and the resulting problem was national--not sectional--and therefore abolition was the responsibility of the whole nation.

Black resistance to slavery was--of necessity--often personal and unlimited--but insofar as opportunity allowed there was always rebellion against slavery. Brown reports an example of such resistance in 1638.

> Mr. Maverick had a Negro woman from whom he was desirous of having a breed of slaves; he therefore ordered his young Negro man to go to bed, when the young

> woman kicked him out, this might have been
> the first case of an insurrection in the
> colonies and it was started by a woman. (14)

Brown reported a series of slave rebellions in the colonies in New York in 1712; South Carolina in 1720; in Rappahannock River, Virginia in 1772; in Savannah, Georgia in 1729; in Williamsburg, Virginia in 1730.

The restive character of the colonial slave population is clearly implied in a document found in Boston. On April 13, 1723, Governor Dummer of Massachusetts issued a proclamation to arrest Negroes and Indians found congregating on the streets of Boston, who were not in the custody of their master or employer. The following preamble describes the rationale behind the proclamation.

> Whereas, within some short time past many
> fires have broke out within the town of
> Boston, and divers buildings have thereby
> been consumed; which fires have been
> designed and industriously kindled by some
> villainous and desperate Negroes, or other
> dissolute people. It being vehemently suspected
> that they have entered into a combination
> to burn and destroy the town, I
> have therefore thought fit, with the advice
> of his majesty's counsel, to issue the
> proclamation. (15)

The discontentment and constant danger of slave uprisings was indicative, argued Brown, that slavery is an unnatural state. Therefore, slave resistance is inevitable and abolition is necessary to resolve the continuing tension and impending disaster.

Originally, the slave masters used religion to keep slaves content but the slaves used religious gatherings or occasions to plant seeds of discontent and to organize means to escape. Therefore, laws were enacted forbidding free blacks and slaves from assembly for religious purposes, without a white overseer.

The Society of Friends was one of the first white organizations to speak out against the sin of human bondage. As early as 1789, the Quakers petitioned congress in favor of the abolition of slavery. Benjamin Lundy, a Quaker, was champion of Negro rights. In 1821, he commenced to publsih a monthly paper called, "The Genius of Universal Emancipation." Lundy's greatest contribution to abolition may have been his influence on William Lloyd Garrison, the founder and publisher of the abolitionist paper called "The Liberator," which commenced on January 1, 1831, in Boston. Two years later, the American Anti-Slavery Society was organized in Philadelphia, Pennsylvania.

Set against the abolitionists were members of the American Colonization Society, which began in 1817. In a subtle manner, it aided the cause of the slaveholders. The primary purpose of the Colonization Society was to carry the free blacks to Africa. Garrison published in 1832, Thoughts on African Colonization, in which he hereby attacked the colonization scheme.

The American Colonization Society was formed by prominent whites, including slaveholders. Its object was to transport free Negroes to Africa on the assumption that they were incapable of serving useful lives in the United States. The Society informed slaveholders that the removal of free Negroes would make more secure the institution of slavery. In short, the Society was formed to protect and perpetuate the institution of slavery. The non-slaveholding members assured the slaveholders that the society would enhance the institution:

> The free people of color are a nuisance to us, and plotters of sedition among your slaves. If they be not speedily removed, your property will be lost, and your lives destroyed.
>
> We therefore do solemnly agree, that if you will unite with us in expelling this dangerous class from our shores, we will never accuse you of robbery or oppression, or irritate your feelings, or identify any one of you as a criminal; but, on the contrary, we will boldly assert your innocence, and applaud you as wise and benevolent men for holding your slaves in subjection until you can cast them out of the country. (16)

The growing opposition to slavery was manifested only in diverse ways which Brown noted. One such was a school which opened for female black women in Canterbury, Connecticut by Miss Prudence Crandall. Prudence Crandall in 1831 established in Canterbury, Connecticut a popular girls' school. The success of the school was short lived when she consented to admit a Negro. The town's people protested, and the white parents withdrew their children from the school. With counsel and support from Garrison, Miss Crandall reopened the school exclusively for Negro girls. The school was outlawed by the Connecticut legislators on the grounds that it would increase the Negro population and this would not be in the best interest of Canterbury. Without the support of law or the town's people, she abandoned the school and departed for Illinois. (See Leon F. Litwack, North of Slavery (Chicago: The University of Chicago Press, 1969), pp. 126-31). David Walker, a black man of Boston, published a potent attack on the institution of slavery which aroused the ire of the pro-slavery feeling of the country. James G. Birney, a prominent minister in Kentucky, freed his slaves and appealed to the slaveholders to follow his example.

The free blacks, especially of Boston, New York, and Philadelphia, were holding annual conventions to recount their grievances and press their claims for emancipation and equal rights. The talents evinced by blacks at these conventions through eloquent speeches and organizational skills enhanced the Negro cause.

Violence exploded in Boston in 1835, when William Lloyd Garrison appeared to attend a meeting of the Ladies Anti-Slavery Society. Garrison had to be taken into prison custody for his personal safety. The New York State Anti-Slavery Society meeting in Utica was attacked by a mob led by a state judge. As a result of his strong appeal against slavery, Reverend Elijah P. Lovejoy (long a particular favorite of Brown) was driven by a mob from St. Louis to Alton, Illinois, where his abolitionist effort expressed in publication continued. A violent mob broke up his printing press and threw it in the river and killed Lovejoy. The blood of the Martyr inspired Wendell Phillips to join the crusade against slavery. During the reign of terror, free blacks were arrested, jailed, shot down, hung from lamp posts, and burned at the stake, but the cry for freedom could not be stopped.

The irrepressible conflict between the north and south was inevitable. The south was determined to secure national support for slavery and in the north there was a growing sentiment to make freedom universal. The politicians were compelled to take sides on the issue.

Brown argued that the "Gag Law," which prohibited the petition on the subject of slavery, the imprisonment of Reverend Charles T. Tarry for aiding slaves to escape, the fugitive slave law of 1850, the "Dred Scott Decision," instead of helping the southern cause, brought its abettors into contempt.

The author also asserted that the religious community could not avoid the question of slavery. The race question did not stop to wait in the vestibule of the churches but entered the sanctuary. Churches north and south had long had what was known as "the Negro-Pew." Brown said, "American Christianity was fashioned to suit the public sentiment." He described the beginning of the independent church movement:

> The first step toward the enjoyment of religious freedman was taken by the colored people of Philadelphia. This was caused by unkind treatment of their white brethren, who considered them a nuisance in their houses of worship, where they were pulled off their knees while in the act of prayer, and ordered to the back seats. From these and other acts of unchristian conduct, the blacks considered it their duty to devise means of having a house for religious worship, of their own. Therefore, in November, 1787, they seceded from a society, built a house to meet in, and set up for themselves. (17)

The whites were uncomfortable worshipping with blacks but they were not content for them to have their separate independent church. Brown wrote: "The whites denied the blacks the right of taking the name Methodist without their consent, and even went so far as to force their white preachers into the pulpits of the colored people on Sundays. The law had more justice in it than the gospel; and it stepped in between the blacks and their religous persecutors and set the former free." Increasingly, the religious situation underscored the rising tension regarding abolition, and Brown's work takes due notice of this fact.

The blacks vindicated their ability to organize and develop their own religious institution through the leadership of Reverend Richard Allen. He built a church in Philadelphia in 1794. The church polity was patterned after the Methodist Church. In 1816, Richard

Allen was ordained Bishop of the African Methodist Episcopal Church. The free blacks in New York were also pressured to organize their own church, and in 1796, under the guidance of Francis Jacobs, William Brown, William Miller, separated from the white Methodist and formed what is known as the African Methodist Episcopal Zion Church.

The independent church movement appealed to other cities such as Baltimore, Richmond, Boston, Providence. The separate church idea surfaced in other denominations such as the Baptist, Presbyterian, and Episcopalian.

In the southern states, the religious liberty of the blacks was more restricted than in the north. Laws were passed to regulate the religious movements of the blacks and deny blacks the right to preach. The assembling of blacks for religious worship was prohibited, unless three or more white persons were present.

The insurrection of the 1820s led the white masters to abandon the widely held view that "true religion" makes good masters and good slaves, and thereafter Negro worship was monitored. At the same time that whites were using religion to teach the blacks to be good slaves, the Negro was using religion as a front for surreptitious activities. With their music, they lulled their slave masters to sleep while their brethren were beating their way to freedom, sometimes to the freedom of the next world, but more often freedom of this world.

The black church movement emerged as a result of restricted and peripheral participation in the white churches. As a result of the separate church movement, the black church was the first community or public organization that Negroes owned and completely controlled. The black church has had a positive effect upon the race because it has been the training ground for developing black leadership and instilling race pride and dignity. Though oblique, the light which the history of the black church throws on the question of abolition nevertheless illuminates the factors which affected the festering conflict.

Brown concluded his book The Rising Son with eighty-one biographical sketches, which is simlar to the final section of his book entitled The Black Man. The author included twenty-eight of the same personalities he included in The Black Man.

The fifty-three new biographical sketches included some noteworthy abolitionists. Information is new--other personalities--<u>but</u> the argument and case are the same. Brown cited the significant contribution of David Ruggles to the anti-slavery movement. He championed the cause of freedom for thirty-five years. The New York resident was one of the founders of the underground railroad. Brown sketched a biography of Jermin W. Loguen who distinguished himself in the underground railroad. In addition to his abolitionist activities, he became a bishop in the A.M.E.Z. Church.

The author cited the distinguished career of Harriet Tubman, alias "Moses." She was born a slave in the south before coming to Boston in 1854. Harriet was invited to the leading abolitionists in the Boston area to tell about the cruelty of slavery in the south. (The scars of human bondage were on her back and shoulders.) Brown represented her as one of the most faithful and daring abolitionists.

The author included a sketch of Lewis Hayden, an abolitionist from his home state of Kentucky. Hayden--as Brown--had spent his early years in slavery. Hayden and his family escaped slavery with the help of a Reverend Calvin Fairbanks and Miss Delia A. Webster, both of whom suffered imprisonment for the kindness extended to the fugitive slaves.

Hayden escaped to Boston where he distinguished himself as an abolitionist and an effective state legislator championing the cause of his people. Regardless of whom the author wrote about in his biographical compilation, they illustrate with various degrees of clarity Brown's unwavering perspective--that slavery is unnatural, indefensible, and unchristian. Therefore it is inevitably doomed, and abolition is a Christian obligation.

William Wells Brown wrote <u>The Negro in the American Rebellion</u> with a feeling of apprehension because he stated in the preface that he had waited patiently, with the hope that some one more competent would take the struggle in hand. He acknowledged his indebtedness to George Livermore's <u>Historical Research</u> and heralded it as "the ablest work ever published on the early history of the Negroes of this country."

As Brown well understood the economic dimensions of slavery, he was aware of the mounting difficulty of achieving his goal, as the growing cotton industry created an expanding demand for slaves. He credited the introduction of Eli Whitney's cotton gin with increasing the value of slave property. With the advent of the need for more labor, it became a widespread consensus that slavery was a necessary evil. In 1790 there were nearly 700,000 slaves in the United States. By 1860 the number had increased to four million, and over three million in the twelve southern states. The religious community softened their earlier opposition to slavery and some even went so far as to defend slavery through the use of scripture.

Brown wrote:

> One of the bitterest fruits of slavery in our land is the cruel spirit of caste, which makes the complexion even of the free Negro a badge of social inferiority, exposing him to insults in the steamboat and railcar, and in all places of public resort, not even excepting the church; banishing him from remunerative occupations; expelling him from the legislatuve hall, the magistrate's bench, and jury box; and crushing his noblest aspirations under a weight of prejudice and proscription which he struggles in vain to throw off. Against this unchristian and hateful spirit, every lover of liberty should enter his solemn protest. This hateful prejudice caused the break up of the school of Miss Prudence Crandall, in the state of Connecticut, in the early days of the anti-slavery agitation. (18)

During the actual prosecution of the war, the cause of abolition and the end of freedom for the slave were inseparably entangled with military and political matters. Brown takes careful note of the complex relation and his attention to personalities often acknowledges specifically, and always argues tacitly for the inseparable relation.

With the impending conflicts and the Confederate army attacking Fort Sumter, April 12, 1861, Lincoln called for 75,000 men to put down the Rebellion. According to Brown, blacks throughout the country offered their services to be told "this is a white man's war and I will never fight by the side of a Nigger," was heard in every quarter where men were seen in Uncle Sam's uniform.

In defiance of strong opposition, blacks were persistent in their effort to win the right and privilege to fight for their freedom. Black men fought for America in the Revolution and the War of 1812. In 1862 Frederick Douglass said sarcastically:

> Colored men were good enough to fight under Washington. They are not good enough to fight under McClellan. They were good enough to fight under Andrew Jackson. They are not good enough to fight under General Halleck. They were good enough to help win American independence, but they are not good enough to help preserve that independence against treason and a rebellion. (19)

Brown gives attention to fact and fancy regarding the fitness and efficiency of blacks as soldiers. He considers prejudices which are not restricted to those who while identified with forces which move toward emancipation sometimes do so with alloyed motives. Yet in case after case the result is the inescapable conclusion that--variously expressed and variously thwarted or assisted--the cause of black freedom is an underlying passion which accounts for the history of the nation and affords a characterization which applies to all blacks.

Brown affirmed that the Emancipation Proclamation gave new life to the Union because black men offered themselves to fight in the Union Army. The new black recruits were received with open arms. Brown argued that blacks played a major role in preserving the Union and winning their freedom.

The Congress passed a bill empowering the President, "to enroll, arm, equip, and receive into the land and naval service of the United States, such a number of volunteers of African descent as he may deem equal to suppress the present rebellion, for such term of service as he may prescribe, not exceeding five years, the colored soldiers were to receive the same rations, clothing and monthly pay as other volunteers." Brown asserted that newly emancipated slaves regarded the use of the musket as the only means of securing their freedom permanently.

The former slaves enlisted in the Union regiments with religious zeal that it was the will of God for them to fight to secure their liberty. Brown reported

Col. T.W. Higginson's account of the prayer of one of his contraband soldiers:

> Let me so lib dat when I die I shall
> hab manners; dat I shall know what to
> say when I see my heavenly Lord.
>
> Let me lib wid de musket in one hand,
> an' de Bible in de order--dat if I die
> at de muzzle of de musket, die in de
> water, die on de land, I may know I hab
> de bressed Jesus in my hand, an' hab
> no fear.
>
> I have lef my wife in de land o bondage;
> my little ones dey say eb'ry night,'Whar
> is my fader?' But when I die, when de
> bressed morning rises, when I shall stan'
> in de glory, wid one foot on de water an'
> one foot on de land, den, O Lord! I
> shall see my wife and my little chil'en
> once more. (20)

Before the emancipation, the planters boasted that their slaves would not bear arms to fight against their former slaveholders. The Battle of Milliken Bend in Mississippi in June of 1863, where the black soldiers fought their ex-slave masters, proved to slave-owners that without a shadow of doubt their charm had gone. Brown reported that the black soldiers fought with courage and conviction.

The Blacks in the north did not volunteer for military duty with the same degree of willingness as the ex-slaves in the south. The black northerners raised the question, "why should we fight?" It was a legitimate question when we consider the fact that every state north of the Mason and Dixon Line, except Massachusetts and Rhode Island, excluded blacks from the jury box, denied them the right to vote, and refused them public education. Brown declared that, "the iron hand of prejudice in the northern states is as circumscribing and unyielding upon him as the manacles that fettered the slaves of the south."

Brown pointed out that northern and western states sympathized with the Rebel states by denying ex-slaves refuge in their states. The position of Illinois stated in "The Daily Alton Democrate" in 1862, is typical of the western and northern states' bias in the matter:

> I hereby give public notice to all free
> Negroes who have arrived here from a
> foreign State within the past two months,
> or may hereafter come into the city of
> Alton with the intention of being resi-
> dents thereof, that they are allowed the
> space of thirty days to remove; and,
> upon failure to leave the city, will,
> after that period, be proceeded against
> by the undersigned, as by law directed.
> The penalty is a heavy fine, to liqui-
> date which the law-officer is compelled
> to offer all free Negroes arrested at
> public auction, unless the fine and all
> costs of suit are promptly paid. I hope
> the city authorities will be spared the
> necessity of putting the above law in
> execution. All railroad companies and
> steamboats are forbidden to land free
> Negroes within the city under the penalty
> of the law. No additional notice will
> be given. Suits will positively be
> instituted against all offenders. (21)

President Lincoln was authorized by Congress to call into service the 54th Regiment of Massachusetts - Voluntary Infantry in 1861. Many of the blacks who volunteered for service had been slaves in the south and had enjoyed the privilege of freedom. Others who joined the 54th Regiment had escaped after the breaking out of the rebellion and most of them had relatives still in bondage.

Major General Hunter, commander over the First Regiment of South Carolina Volunteers, concluded, after his initial experience with black soldiers, that successful prosecution of the war lies in the unlimited employment of black troops. The officer discerned that black soldiers were superior to white soldiers because they were more familiar with the terrain. Their peculiarities of temperament, position, and motive set the black soldiers apart from the white soldiers. "Instead of leaving their homes and families to fight, they are fighting for their homes and families."

T.W. Higginson, Col. Com. First Regiment of South Carolina wrote the following evaluation of the black soldiers:

> Everything, even to the piloting of the
> vessel, and the selection of the proper

> points for cannonading, was done by my
> soldiers; indeed, the real conductor of the
> whole expedition at the St. Mary's River was
> a man of extraordinary qualities, who
> needs nothing but knowledge of the alpha-
> bet to entitle him to the most signal
> promotion. In every instance where I
> follow his advice, the predicted result
> followed; and I never departed from it,
> however slightly, without having reason
> for subsequent regret. (22)

Captain Andre Callioux was a black soldier who distinguished himself as a warrior for the regiment in Louisiana. He was well educated, polished in manners and a splendid horseman. He petitioned to lead his troops in the most dangerous battle.

Brown recorded the Battle of Poison Springs, Arkansas when the Union Army and rebel troops were involved in fierce fighting. Six hundred of the Union forces were blacks from Kansas. Many of the black soldiers were disciples of John Brown. The black troops distinguished themselves as courageous soldiers. They went into battle singing the following song:

> Old John Brown's body lies a mouldering
> the grave. While weep the sons of bondage,
> whom he ventured to save; But though he lost
> his life in struggle for the slave, His
> soul is marching on. Glory, glory, Hallelujah!
> Glory, glory, Hallelujah, Glory, glory Halla-
> lujah, His soul is marching on! (23)

Brown saw the legacy of slavery and discrimination reflected in the inequalities inflicted upon black soldiers. The black soldiers were promised the same treatment, clothing and pay as white soldiers. The black soldiers were paid less than the white soldier and were denied clothing. Brown was sensitive to all the implications of blacks in the army, but he was also aware of the enormity of the race problem as it assumed overwhelming dimensions when the war was over--abolition was far more than legal freedom and in a way was a more remote goal after emancipation than before.

After Appomattox, the south was determined to reduce the blacks to a state of serfdom, if they could not have them as slaves. The significance of Brown's analysis indicates his understanding that the burden under which the slaves had struggled in north and south alike was more than slavery (which has been legally outlawed) and not susceptible to resolution through legislation. He sensed the deep roots of the human determination to keep--or recapture--power, and the jeopardy in which any freedom always exists. The south remembered that when the secessionists withdrew from the Union in 1860, Andrew Johnson had said, "If I were president I would try them for treason, and, if convicted I would hang them."

When Johnson succeeded Lincoln, therefore, a committee from the south went to confer with the new president in an effort to reinstate his enemies in his good graces.

> We have, in the past, been your political opponents. In the future, we shall be your friends; because we now see that you were right, and we were wrong. We ask, nay, we beg you to permit us to reconstruct the Southern States. Our people, south, are loyal to a man, and wish to return at once to their relations in the General Government. We look upon you Mr. President, as the embodiment of the truly chivalrous southerner, one who, born and bred in the south, understands her people; to you we appeal for justice; for we are sure that your impulses are pure. At the next presidential election, the south will be a unit for the man who saves her from the hands of these Yankees, who now, under the protection of the Freedman's Bureau, are making themselves right. Your genius and sagacity, and your unequalled statesmanship mark you out as the father of his country. (24)

President Johnson was impressed with the southerners' appeal and pledged to lay their case before the cabinet. The chairman of the southern committee gave an immediate response:

> We do not appeal to the cabinet, it is to you, Mr. President, that we come. Were you a common man, we should expect you to ask advice of your cabinet; but we regard you as master, and your secretaries as your servants. You are capable of acting without consulting them; we thank the

Andrew Jackson of today. (25)

Brown wrote that the southern committee requested the president to punish the rebellious traitors by giving them an office. He pointed out that St. Paul had said, "If thine enemy hunger, feed him, if he thirst, give him drink: for in so doing, thou shalt heap coals of fire on his head." Brown continued sarcastically that the former enemies of the president were now hungry for office, and thirsty for the good liquor they used to get in the congressional saloons.

Shortly after the southern committee had talked with the president, a committee of black men, consisting of Frederick Douglass, William Whipper, George T. Downing and L.H. Douglass, conferred with the president. Downing was an erudite New Englander, who addressed the president as follows:

> We come to you in the name of the United States, and we are delegated to come by some who have unjustly worn iron manacles on their bodies; by some whose minds have been manacled by class legislation. We are Americans. We are citizens. We see no recognition of color or race in the organic law of the land. It knows no privileged class, and therefore we cherish the hope that we may be fully enfranchised, not only here in this district, but throughout the land. (26)

Frederick Douglass addressed the president as follows:

> Mr. President, we are not here to enlighten you, sir, as to your duties as the chief magistrate of the republic, but to show our respect and to present in brief the claims of our race to your favorable consideration. In the order of divine Providence, you are placed in a position where you have the power to save or destroy us, to bless or blast us--I mean our whole race. Your noble and human predecessor placed in our hands the sword, to assist in saving the nation; and we do hope that you, his able successor, will favorably regard the placing in our hands the ballot with which to save ourselves. The fact that we subjects of government, and subject to taxation, subject to volunteer in the service

> of the country, subject to being drafted,
> subject to bear the burden of the state,
> makes it not improper that we should ask
> to share in the privilege of this
> condition. (27)

Brown did not record the president's reply because he called it "illogical and untrue." Brown argued that the president was intellectually inferior to the able black delegation. In general the president's response was one of explaining and justifying the hostility which exist between the black and white in the south. The president viewed the problem as primarily a class struggle between the ex-slaves and the poor whites.

Brown argued that southerners following the war regarded themselves as overpowered but not conquered. He accused the Andrew Johnson administration of creating an atmosphere for reinstating the Negro-whipping post and allowing old slave masters to kill their former slaves in open daylight. A black man named Jordan opened a school for blacks in Tennessee; he was punished and was told by a white soldier, "If you want to go to heaven you must pray; for you can't get there by teaching the Niggers. We can't go to school, and I'll be damned if Niggers shall."

In short, Brown concluded that the Emancipation Proclamation and the Civil Right Bill were almost dead letters. The southern confederacy compelled the national government to abolish chattel slavery in self-defense. Following the war, the southern states had fallen into the hands of the former slaveholders. Brown said, "If a man has no vote for the men and the measures which tax himself, his family and his property, and all which determines his reputation, that man is still a slave." He observed corectly that the proclamation removed the chains, but still there was no recognition of their rights for self-improvement. The ultimate goal of abolition, often stated and always implied in the anti-slavery effort, had been only partially achieved.

CHAPTER VI

A MIGHTY PEN

William Wells Brown's commitment to the struggle for freedom and equality for the blacks was a consuming passion that found expression, not alone in effort to effect his goals through legislation and political activity. He expressed himself, as well, in the idiom of literature.

Brown continued his relentless endeavor to crusade against slavery through writing novels and plays. He is recognized as the first black American male to publish a novel and a play. His first novel entitled Clotel, or The President's Daughter, was published in 1853, and a revised version, called Clotelle: A Tale of the Southern States, was published in 1864. In his original version, Thomas Jefferson is the father of the slave heroine in his novel. The president's name was offensive to some of the abolitionist sympathizers. To broaden the appeal, Brown substituted an "unnamed senator" for the name of President Jefferson. The revised edition had also the expressed purpose of entertaining the Union Army in their quest for "Universal Emancipation."

After experiencing the horrors of slavery and delight in freedom, Brown expressed empathy with the slaves in a poem in the preface of his novel:

> Is true freedom but to break;
> Fetters for our own dear sake,
> And with leathern hearts forget;
> No, true freedom is to share!
> All the chains our brothers wear, and with heart
> And hand to be earnest to make others free. (28)

The novel touches on slavery in Richmond, Natchez, New Orleans, and in areas along the Ohio and Mississippi Rivers. The plot treats a situation all too familiar in the ante-bellum south. The heroine, Clotel, is the daughter of one of the first families of the region. Clotel resided in Richmond, Virginia. Earlier she had lived with members of her family; but Currer, Clotel's Mother, was sold to a resident modeled after James Walker, the notorious slave trader of Natchez, Mississippi. Althea, the sister of Clotel, was purchased by a slaveholder in New Orleans, Louisana.

In the novel the sale of the two heroines was advertised in a Richmond newspaper:

> Thirty eight Negroes will be offered for sale on Monday, November 10, at twelve o'clock, being the entire stock of the late John Graves, Esq. Also several mulatto girls of rare personal qualities; two of them very superior. Any gentleman or lady wishing to purchase can take any of the above slaves on trial for a week. (29)

The two referred to in the advertisement as "very superior" were Clotel and Althea. While Currer was the official property of John Graves, Esq., she also served as the housekeeper of a "young slaveholder named Thomas Jefferson." Jefferson--having taken Currer as a mistress, at least on occasion--had, according to Brown, fathered her two daughters, Clotel and Althea. Jefferson moved from Virginia to Washington to serve the government but he left Currer and their two daughters behind in Richmond. Following the departure of Jefferson, Currer was hired out by her master as a laundress. Currer was industrious and proud and she made every effort to instill the dignity of womanhood in her daughters.

According to Brown, "nearly all the Negro parties in the cities and towns of the southern states are made up of quadroon and mulatto girls and white men." The beautiful daughters of Currer attracted much attention at these parties. It was at one of these gatherings that Clotel won the admiration of Horatio Green. At the time Horatio met Clotel he was a college student. He frequently visited Currer's house to see her daughter. Green promised to purchase Clotel for his mistress and to provide her with a home. Clotel awaited the fulfillment of Horatio's promise with great anticipation.

> It was a beautiful moonlight night in August, when all who reside in tropical climes are eagerly grasping for a breath of fresh air, that Horatio Green was seated in the small garden behind Currer's cottage, with the object of his affections by his side. And it was here that Horatio drew from his pocket the newspaper, wet from the press, and read the advertisement for the sale of the slaves to which

we have alluded; Currer and her two daughters
being of the number. At the close of the
evening's visit, and as the young man was
leaving, he said to the girl, "you shall
soon be free and your own mistress." (30)

Horatio purchased Clotel at a public slave auction
for fifteen hundred dollars. Brown observed that the
sale of Clotel occurred in a southern city "thronged
with churches...and whose ministers preach that slavery
is a God-ordained institution!"

Horatio provided his slave mistress with a beautiful cottage on the outskirts of Richmond. Clotel was
conscious of the fact that her relationship with Horatio
had no legal sanction. "If the mutual love we have for
each other, and the dictates of your affections fall
from me," she told Horatio, "I would not, if I could,
hold you by a single fetter." To this union was born
a baby daughter, named Mary. The child brought new
happiness and joy to their home. Clotel was sensitive
to the hostility of a slave society and the possibility of her returning to slavery and separation from
her child. To escape the restriction and cruelties of
American slavery, Clotel asked "Horatio to remove to
France or England, where both [sic] and her child
would be free, and where colour was not a crime,"
Horatio did not oppose the idea in principle but his
political aspirations overpowered Clotel's proposal.

> He still loved Clotel, but he was now
> becoming engaged in political and other
> affairs which kept him oftener and
> longer from the young mistress, and
> ambition to become a statesman was
> slowly gaining ascendancy over him. (31)

To enhance his political career, Horatio arranged
a diplomatic marriage with the daughter of one of the
wealthiest and most influential families in Richmond.
When Clotel heard of Horatio's approaching marriage
she despaired. The novel then becomes a tragic portrayal in the brutal melodramatic tradition that figures
so largely in the abolitionist literature of the times.
The form is naturalistic. Like Uncle Tom's Cabin it
owes much to Oliver Twist and the works of Charles
Dickens. Clotel, like Eliza, is a mulatto, a tragic
character, for whom we sympathize more because she is
part white than because she is colored. The quadroon
is tarred by her slave ancestry; and she represents

the irrational persecution brought about by a color caste.

For Brown, Clotel becomes the stock method of abolitionist propaganda. His characters are clear-cut, simple and artificial. They make natural vehicles for moral extremes, cast as either right (Clotel) or wrong (Horatio). Action is emphasized to the expense of in-depth depiction of character. In all charity Clotel and other characters are stereotypes in a stable, moral and fanciful world.

Brown's moral thus contains the well-used triangle of hero, heroine and villain. The plot material does not venture beyond the excitement of miscegenation and slavery's oppressive features, since the moral natures of hero and villain are fixed and without possibility of development. There is no inner conflict. The reader is sustained by the thriller-like aspect of the story in action revolving about a romantic projection between the classes. And Clotel is fully a novel of social aspiration as much as it is propaganda.

The period of the novel is well after the importation of African slaves had ceased in the United States. The slave had to structure his life in a culture to which he was denied full access. The process of assimilation was deliberately obstructed by whips. And shortly after American independence was won there were Afro-Americans who were native Americans by several generations.

By this time, too, Clotel's people were already losing their racial identity. Countless white males had been trying to wash her whole race whiter than snow. There was even a premium on "white slaves." This illegitimate offspring was creating new problems and moral ambiguities. From the start miscegenation was the congenital weakness in slavery's biological defense.

In Brazil and Cuba the importation of African slaves replenished the attrition of slaves lost to biological assimilation. But in North America manumission from interracial liaisons was legally impossible. But interracial ancestry created a privileged group of mulatto house servants, thereby resulting in a division of labor that corresponded to complexion.

In Brown's view the color line, and not just

slavery, is unjust because it suppresses natural human instincts of affection. His novel is an argument for freedom and also for assimilation. For Currer, the mulatto mistress of President Thomas Jefferson, is just like other white mistresses. She is attractive and an expert laundress. Her children, Clotel and Althea, are descendant of quality, as much like "cultured" and refined white women as possible. After Clotel is sold, her jealous white mistress makes the slave cut off her beautiful hair. The edict for Clotel to cut her hair won the approval of the other slaves. After her hair was cut, the other servants laughed, "Miss Clo needn't strut round so big, she got nappy har well as I," said Nell, with a broad grin that showed her teeth.

"She tinks she white, when she come here wid dat long har of hers," replied Mill.

"Yes," continued Nell; "Missus make her take down her wool so she no put it up today."

Brown observed that Clotel's fair complexion was despised with envy by the other servants as well as the white mistress. In addition to the hostilities Clotel encountered, she was still grief-stricken over the separation from her only child, Mary. The heartfelt grief of Clotel was perceived by her master and her refusal to eat caused him to sell her to a young man for housekeeper.

The audience for Clotel was the parochial one of the dime store novel. It appealed to the new literate class of quality white folks and freedmen. Brown's aim was not to attack the character of Thomas Jefferson but to exploit an entertaining story as an argument against American slavery.

Brown's novel is an anthology of anti-slavery material which he employs to expose the tragedy of human bondage. "The blood of the first Amercan statesmen coursing through the veins of the slaves" is a central theme of the novel. The increasing mulatto population of slaves caused Henry Clay to predict that the abolition of slavery would be brought about by the amalgamation of the races. The careers of Currer and her two daughters demonstrate that slaves, regardless of physical attraction and ability, are entirely subject to the will of their master. The institution of slavery is sanctioned by law, and even the religious leaders are mere echoes of public sentiment rather than correctors of wrongs perpetrated by human bondage.

Brown's writings demonstrate that the members of slave families encountered tremendous emotional suffering and stress. Brown cited in his autobiography that his mother had seven children fathered by seven different men. The major decisions and provisions for the slave family were made by the master, and the slave father was left with little or no authority. The master's lust for pretty black women jeopardized the development of family morality and stability.

The fear of separation from their loved ones caused many slaves not to want to establish family ties. Rather than see their loved ones beaten, insulted, overworked and abused, many slaves preferred living on a different plantation from their mates. Henry Bibb felt that way: "If my wife must be exposed to the insults and licentious passions of wicked slavedrivers and overseers; if she must bear the stripes of the lash laid on by an unmerciful tyrant; if this is to be done with impunity, which is frequently done by slaveholders and their abettors, Heaven forbid that I should be compelled to witness the sight."

From the accounts of Brown and other fugitive slave narrators, slaves were made to feel inferior and degraded from the cradle to the grave.

The inherent limitations of Brown's melodrama are sketchiness in the development of the plots and in the portrayal of characters. Of necessity his story foundered within the artistic framework of 19th century Romanticism. At the same time, Clotel detracted nothing from the horrors of slavery as Brown had witnessed them. It is the most important of his works with the exception of his own narrative. As a publishing venture Clotel was unspectacular. Published the year after Uncle Tom's Cabin, Brown's novel could only suffer by comparison.

Although its shelf life was brief, Clotel was widely read and received positive reviews in England and among anti-slavery critics. To paraphrase Charles Sumner, romance has no story of more thrilling interest than his. Classical antiquity has preserved no examples of adventurous trial more worthy of renown. His novel goes to the heart of men.

CHAPTER VII

HIGH PROPAGANDA

Brown also employed the use of drama to continue his exploits against the institution of slavery. Originally the author wrote "The Escape, Or, A Leap for Freedom" for personal satisfaction and the private consideration of personal friends. After Brown read the drama before a literary society, he was encouraged to publish the play. It was published in 1858, and Brown has been acclaimed the first black author to publish a drama. As the author had done repeatedly in other works, he reminded the reader that he owed the public no apology for errors because he was born in slavery, and never had a day's schooling in his life.

Instead of describing slavery in the south, as he had done in Clotel, Brown, in Escape, reminded the reader of slavery in the mid-west. The slave setting in his drama is a small farm near St. Louis, Missouri. Many of the features and episodes were true and drawn from his own experience. The central theme of the drama, predictably, was a potent anti-slavery argument.

The main character is a slave master, Dr. Gaines, who is a politician and physician. He is the proprietor of Poplar Farm, located near St. Louis, and widely acclaimed for its beautiful slave women. The white couple, Dr. and Mrs. Gaines, talk Christian sentiments while threatening to whip their slaves. When a clergyman, Reverend John Pinchen, visits Mrs. Gaines, he recalls a dream he has had of Paradise and of old friends he visited there. The slave Hannah asks him, "Massa Pinchen, did you see my ole man Ben up dar in hebben?" The ensuing dialogue is blatant, but nevertheless telling:

> Mr. Pinchen: No Hannah: I didn't go amongst the niggers.
>
> Mr. Gaines: No, of course Brother Pinchen didn't go among the Blacks, what are you asking questions for? Never mind, my lady, I'll whip you well when I am done here. I'll skin you from head to foot. [Aside] Do go on with your heavenly discourse, Brother Pinchen. It does my very soul good, this is indeed a precious moment for me. I love to hear Christ and Him crucified. (32)

The heroine of the drama is Melinda, a slave who is greatly fancied by her slave master, Dr. Gaines. The physician provides a place for her to stay on a remote plantation, where he can make her his mistress. The slave hero is Glen who is the property of Dr. Gaines' brother-in-law. For some time, Melinda had been in love with Glen whom she has secretly married in a moonlight ceremony officiated by the plantation slave preacher.

Marriage among slaves, except by the kind of pledge exchanged by Glen and Melinda, was unknown.

> Glen. How slowly the time passes away. I've been waiting here two hours, and Melinda has not yet come. What keeps her, I cannot tell. I waited long and late for her last night, and when she approached, I sprang to my feet, caught her in my arms, pressed her to my heart, and kissed away the tears from her moistened cheeks. She placed her trembling hand in mine, and said, "Glen, I am yours, I will never be the wife of another." I clasped her to my bosom, and called God to witness that I would ever regard her as my wife. Old Uncle Joseph joined us in holy wedlock by moonlight; that was the only marriage ceremony. I looked upon the vow as ever-binding on me, for I am sure that a just God will sanction our union in heaven. Still, this man, who claims Melinda as his property, is unwilling for me to marry the woman of my choice, because he wants her himself. But he shall not have her. What he will say when he finds that we are married, I cannot tell; but I am determined to protect my wife or die. Ah! here comes Melinda. (33)

Dr. Gaines offered to buy Glen a new suit of clothing if he would give up on Melinda. Glen reported his response to Dr. Gaines' request to Melinda:

> I answered, that, while I love life better than death, even life itself could not tempt me to consent to a separation that would make life an unchanging curse. Oh, I would kill myself, Melinda, if I thought that, for the sake of life, I could consent to your

degredation. No, Melinda, I can die, but shall
never live to see you the Mistress of another
man.

Melinda courageously endures the Gaines' blandishments but makes it known to her unscrupulous master that she entertains a contempt for him.

Sir, I am your slave, you can do as you
please with the avails of my labor, but
you shall never tempt me to swerve from
the path of virtue. (34)

Mrs. Gaines senses her husband's duplicity and insists that the "mulatto wench" be sold out of her sight. Leading her to believe that he has sold Melinda, Dr. Gaines hides her in a cottage in seclusion. The following evening, the physician visits Melinda, and quizzes her about Glen. Dr. Gaines reminds her:

Now, Melinda, that black scoundrel Glen
has been putting these notions into your
head. I'll let you know that you are my
property and I'll do as I please with you.
I'll teach you there are no limits to my
power. (35)

With fierce honesty, Melinda informs the physician that she is married to Glen. Dr. Gaines vows to purchase Glen from his brother-in-law, and when he has acquired him as his property, to whip him into submission. Dr. Gaines has exited just in time to avoid meeting his furious wife, whose suspicions and jealousy have brought her to Melinda's cottage. In a dramatic scene, the master's wife attempts to force Melinda to drink poison and chases her with a knife. Melinda defends herself and drives Mrs. Gaines out of her cottage.

Immediately after buying Glen, Dr. Gaines goads the young man into attacking him, and thus succeeds in casting him into prison. In the dungeon, Glen reflected:

When I think of my ummerited sufferings,
it almost drives me mad. I struck the
doctor, and for that I must remain here
loaded with chains. But why did he strike
me? He takes my wife from me, sends her
off, and then comes and beats me over

> the head with his cane. I did right to
> strike him back again. I wish I had killed
> him. Oh! There is a volcano pent up in the
> hearts of the slaves of these Southern
> States that will burst forth ere long. I
> would be willing to die, if I could smite
> down with these chains every man who attempts
> to enslave his fellow man. (36)

It is Sampey, a house slave, who informs Glen about the whereabouts of his wife. Sampey had been a cause of embarrassment to Gaines when a house guest remarked, "Madam, I should have known this was the Colonel's son [that is, Dr. Gaines], if I had met him in California; for he looks so much like his papa." Meanwhile, Dr. Gaines sends Mr. Scragg, his ruthless overseer, to whip his unruly slave, Glen. The overseer is so elated with his assignment that he says he "would rather whip that Nigger than go to heaven."

Glen, however, overpowers Mr. Scragg, and the following night is accidentally reunited with Melinda.

> I escaped from the overseer, whom Dr. Gaines
> sent to flog me. Yes, I struck him over the
> head with his own club, and I made the wine
> flow freely; yes, I pounded his old skillet
> well for him, and then jumped out of the win-
> dow. It was a leap for freedom. Yes,
> Melinda, it was a leap for freedom. I've
> said "master" for the last time. I am free;
> I'm bound for Canada. Come, let's be off,
> at once, for the Negro dogs will be put upon
> our track. Let us once get beyond the Ohio
> River, and all will be right. (37)

The fugitives did not reach Canada (freedom) without a struggle. There were moments when Melinda was tired and hungry and questioned whether freedom was worth the hardship they had to endure.

The drama closes with Dr. Gaines, the slave owner; Mr. Scragg, the overseer; and Cato, the happy-go-lucky slave in pursuit of Melinda and Glen. Cato was reputed as another loyal servant of Dr. Gaines. He has been trusted by Dr. Gaines to "doctor" other slaves. While the slave catcher's party sleeps in an Ohio hotel, Cato, dressed in Dr. Gaines' clothes, leaps to his own freedom.

> Cato: I allers knowed I was a doctor, an'
> now de ole boss has put me at it. I muss
> change my coat. Ef any niggers come, I
> wants to look suspectable. Dis jacket don't
> suit a doctor; I'll change it. Ah! now I
> look like a doctor. Now I can bleed, pull
> teef, or cut off a leg. Oh! well, ef I ain't
> put de pills stuff on the entment stuff
> togedder, by golly, dat ole cuss will be mad
> when he finds it out, won't he?...Ah! Yonder
> comes Mr. Campell's Pete an' Ned; dems de
> ones massa said was coming. I'll see ef I
> looks right. [Goes to the looking-glass
> and views himself.] I em some punkins, ain't
> I? (38)

Glen and Melinda, as well as the good Cato who knows how to please while despising his master, escape to Canada with the help of northern abolitionists. The last scene takes place in a barroom in the American Hotel, while Glen and Melinda were waiting for a boat. A fight erupts between pro-slavery and anti-slavery factions of ferries crossing the river to Canada.

> Cato: I wonder if dis is me? By golly, I
> is free as a frog. But maybe I is mistaken;
> maybe dis ain't me. Cato, is dis you? Yes,
> seer. Well, now it is me, an' I'm a free
> man. But, stop! I muss change my name, Rose
> ole massa might foller me, and somebody might
> tell him dat dey seed Cato; so I'll change my
> name, and den he won't know me if he sees me.
> Now, what shall I call myself? I'm now in a
> suspectable part of de country, an' I muss
> have a suspectable name. Ah! I'll call my-
> self Alexander Washington Napoleon Pompey
> Caesar. Dar, now, dat's a good long, suspec-
> table name, and everybody will suspect me.
> (39)

One of those involved in the fight is a Mr. White, a citizen of Massachusetts, who thanks God that he is from a free state and thinks slavery the worst sin a man can commit. He is accused of talking treason. When he claims that the Constitution gives the right to speak his sentiments, his opponents argue: "We don't care for Constitutions nor nothin' else. We made the Constitution, and we'll break it."

The curtain closes with a lively fight in which Mr. White fights off the Mississippi villains--with his umbrella. Glen, Melinda, and Cato, leaping into the boat just as it pulls away from the shore, are shouting loudly for freedom as the curtain falls or reading ends.

Brown was an unrelenting crusader, and kept the flame of freedom burning through the struggle for Negro equality which followed emancipation. In 1880, Brown published My Southern Home, Or The South and Its People. The book was written thirty years after Three Years in Europe and seventeen years after the end of the Civil War. The first fifteen chapters of the book repeat both ideas and incidents found in Clotel, The Escape, Narratives, and The Negro in the American Rebellion.

The remaining thirteen chapters are devoted to the question of Negro equality. Brown, unlike many abolitionists, did not end his crusade for freedom when the Emancipation Proclamation was signed. Brown maintained that the task of the abolitionist was incomplete because the federal government confused Negro citizenship with social equality. Brown attempted to clarify the position of the Negro in the following statement:

> Social equality is a condition of society that must make itself. There are colored families residing in every Southern State, whose education and social position is far above a large portion of their neighboring whites. To compel them to associate with these whites would be a grievous wrong. Then, away with this talk, which is founded in hatred to an injured people. Give the colored race in the south equal protection before the law, and then we say to them--"now, to gain the social prize, paddle your own canoe." (40)

The poor and uneducated whites were most vulnerable to the fears and distortions of social equality. Brown insisted that whites were "more afraid of the Negroes' ability and industry than of his color rubbing off against them." In some ways, the institution of slavery had equipped the ex-slave to be better prepared for employment than his white counterpart. Domestic slavery exposed the Negroes to the culture which gave them training and experience superior to the poor and uneducated whites.

It was necessary to continue to press the

abolitionist cause because the government emancipated the Negroes without protecting the ex-slaves from the hostility of their former slave masters. Brown maintained that Negro citizenship entitled the full protection under the constitution. From the author's travels through the south in 1879, he noted that blacks were the victims of intimidation and assassination by the Ku Klux Klan and white leaguers. In brief, Brown concluded that the reign of terror which pervaded the south had returned the Negroes to chattel slavery. In states such as Mississippi, Georgia, South Carolina, Louisiana, Alabama, and Florida where blacks should have had political power, they had little or no voice in either state or national government.

Brown maintains that in defiance of almost insurmountable obstacles, the blacks did make a significant contribution in state and national politics. He wrote that state legislatures during Reconstruction were

> ...composed mainly of colored men. The few whites that were there were not only of no help to the blacks, but it would have been better for the character of the latter and the country at large, if most of them had been in some state prison. Colored men went into the legislatures somewhat as children go for the first time to a sabbath school. Many had been elected by constituencies of which not more than ten in a hundred could read the ballots; These representatives could not write their own name. (41)

Brown hastened to point out that blacks were ill trained and inexperienced because they were the product of the institution of slavery. The deplorable conditions in the south after the war indicated that slavery was detrimental to the former slaveholders as well as the ex-slaves. Brown maintained that the former slaves "reconstructed the state governments that their masters had destroyed, became legislators, held state offices, and with all their blunders, surpassed the whites that had preceded them," and said that "future generations would marvel at the calm forbearance, good sense, and Christian zeal of the American Negro of the 19th Century."

The struggle for freedom did not end with the signing of the emancipation because it could not eradicate a slave mentality. The work of abolition could not cease as long as there was inward bondage on the part of the ex-slave and former slaveholders. Brown was careful to point out the responsibilities which go along with freedom.

After the Civil War, the blemish of inherent Negro inferiority and racial prejudice continued to thwart the Negroes' struggle for equality and full citizenship. Brown continued his crusade for freedom by shifting his emphases from abolition of slavery to economics, self-help and racial pride as the basics for achieving black equality. He maintained that through the acquisition of wealth, education, and morality, blacks would demand respect of whites and thus be accorded their full rights as citizens. He admonished blacks following the Civil War to embrace the Protestant ethics of thrift, land ownership, and industry as the key elements necessary to attain full equality.

> We need more self-reliance, more confidence in the ability of our people; more manly independence, a higher standard of moral, social and literary culture...while the barriers of prejudice keep us morally and socially from being educated by white society, we must make a strong effort to raise ourselves from the common level where emancipation and the new order of things found us. (42)

Freedom, according to Brown, should be an inherent gift from birth but each person should earn his own social equality. He warned blacks that "the last struggle for our rights; the battle for our own civilization, is entirely with ourselves, and the problem is to be solved by us."

Cooperation, coordination and organization, Brown insisted, were the main ingredients for complete emancipation. History teaches us that all civilized races have risen by means of combination and cooperation. The European immigrants who arrived in America as destitutes by individual initiative and group cooperation gained social equality. In contrast to the European immigrants, who brought rich culture and long histories with them, the Negro slaves were completely stripped of their past. Brown reminds us that we must not forget that Negroes are descendants of slaves and European immigrants are not.

> In America, the Negro stands alone as a
> race. No people has borne oppression
> like the Negro, and no race has been so
> much imposed upon. Whatever progress he
> makes, it must be mainly by his own
> efforts. (43)

The Emancipation Proclamation did not change the public mind about the false theory of the inherent inferiority of the Negro. The long ordeal of slavery and racial prejudice left some Negroes with a false sense of inferiority and some whites with a false sense of superiority. Brown explained, "that the black man's position as a servant, for many generations, has not only made the other races feel that it is his legitimate sphere, but he himself feels more at home in a white apron and a towel on his arm than...with a quill behind his ear and a ledger before him."

Brown recognized the dignity and respect in all honest work. He was critical of menial labor on the grounds that Negroes were confined to servitude because of racial prejudice. Brown took the position that a person, regardless of race, should be free to work in whatever trade or profession his education, inclination and ability will support. He cautioned blacks against selecting a trade or profession for the sake of holding a prestigious title or position.

> An honorable, lucrative, and faithful earned
> professional reputation, is a career of
> honesty, patience, sobriety, toil and
> Christian zeal. (44)

The legacy of slavery left both the ex-slave and former slaveholders ill prepared for their new-found freedom. In addition to cooperation, coordination and organization, Brown argued that education was another important element in the Negroes' struggle for full equality. He encouraged black educators from the north to go south to train their black brothers and sisters. Brown contended that white teachers were at a decisive disadvantage trying to teach blacks because of their inability to transcend their racial biases.

> It is generally known that all the white
> teachers in our colored schools feel
> themselves above their work; and the
> fewest number have any communication
> whatever with their pupils that under
> no circumstances were they to recognize or

speak to them on the street. (45)

The unyielding patron of self-discipline, self-reliance, self-confidence and self-improvement believed that blacks could not afford the luxuries of idleness and slothfulness. Brown supported organizing literary societies for the expressed purpose of developing the mind through reading and the exchange of intellectual ideas. He promoted and encouraged black scholarship. He was one of the first of his race to encourage blacks to write and produce their own literature. Brown admonished blacks to be supportive of each other by patronizing their own businesses and thinking positively about black enterprises. Brown advocated putting the principles of cooperation and self-reliance into practice by encouraging blacks to buy and support each other in business. These principles of cooperation and self-reliance must be applied by blacks supporting each other in business. Rather than raise questions concerning the possibility of a black business being successful, Blacks should make it live through their patronage and support.

Brown contended the black economic development was necessary to demand respect and equality. He cited the Jews as an example; they did not gain respectability until they gained economic independence. William Lloyd Garrison, also, underscored the importance of Negroes accumulating wealth, because "money begets influence and respectability." Delegates at a Negro Convention in 1848 echoed the same sentiment: "To be dependent is to be degraded. Men may indeed pity us but they cannot respect us--at least, not until the negro won economic independence for himself and cease to rely on the white for the necessities of life."

To attain economic independence, Brown exhorted Blacks to "cultivate self denial." Blacks must learn to be thrifty and live within their means by curbing their appetites for luxuries.

> Go to our churches on the sabbath, and see the silk, the satin, the velvet, and the costly feathers, and talk with the uneducated wearers, and you will see at once the main hindrance of self-elevation. (46)

Long before the Martin Luther King, Stokely Carmichael and Malcolm X Era, Brown embraced the concept of racial pride and identity as the main ingredients for black liberation and integration. The institution of slavery formulated and promulgated the concept that Negroes had no culture of their own or, if they did, that it was both different from and inferior to that of the whites. The pro-slavery apologist argued that their skin color was a badge of inferiority. It was inevitable that the cruelties of slavery would leave Negroes with a distorted image of themselves. Therefore, long before it was fashionable, Brown exhorted Negroes to be "Black and Proud."

He gave special articulation to the sentiment in a sequence in My Southern Home.

"Don't call me a Negro; I'm an American," said a black to me a few days since. "Why not?" I asked.

"Well sir, I was born in this country, and don't want to be called out of my name."

"Just then, an Irish-American came up, and shook hands with me. He had been a neighbor of mine in Cambridge. When the young man was gone, I inquired of the black man what he thought the man was:

"Oh!" replied he, "he is an Irishman."

"What makes you think so?" I inquired.

"Why, his brogue is enough to tell it."

"Then," said I, "Why is not your color enough to tell that you're a Negro?"

"Arh!" said he, "That's a horse of another color, and left me with a Ha, ha ha!"

Racial pride, solidarity, self-help and self-identification are basic steps in the Negroes' struggle for integretaion. Ultimately Brown was an integrationist who believed that all ethnic entities had something distinct to contribute to the totality of American culture and should be accorded full participation in American society. However, the complexity of the race problem deemed it necessary for Brown to appear inconsistent and ambivalent in his racial ideology. At one moment he favored racial solidarity and in another he espoused its infeasibility. The sense of "twoness" as W.E.B. Dubois called it, the dual identification with race and nation, was a fundamental quality in Brown's racial ideology. Nevertheless, he made it quite obvious that his ultimate goal for the Negro is full citizenship and integration.

In his fictive and dramatic works, Brown has progressed from simply showing the horror of slavery by describing it, to giving an analysis of the complexity of the racial situation. He was sensitive to the fact that the emancipation would not settle the struggle for freedom and equality. He observed that the emancipation freed the slave but ignored the problem of Negro equality. Brown contended that as long as blacks were denied equal opportunities in employment, education, public accommodation and government, the Negro was not free and the crusade for equality must continue. He reminded the ex-slaves that they could not afford the luxuries of idleness and slothfulness. Brown exhorted blacks to continue the struggle for equality through self-discipline, self-reliance, self-confidence, and self-improvement.

CHAPTER VIII

THE COLOR OF HAM AND CAIN

William Wells Brown, a productive and published writer of American literature, was one of the first black American authors to support himself through writing. He first published in 1847, only thirteen years after his escape from human bondage. Over the next forty years, Brown published nine major books and at his death in 1884, his works had appeared in over thirty editions. Primarily known as a writer, he was also an effective lecturer for the abolition of slavery.

Brown's initial publication, his The Narrative of William Wells Brown, was an effective attack upon slavery. His narrative was widely read and over a two-year period, 8,000 copies (four editions) were sold. The slave narrative presented the side of slavery as seen by its victims. To make a fair-minded and objective appraisal of American slavery, it is imperative to hear the side of the slave as well as the slave master. It is as important to know what the institution meant to Brown the slave, as what it meant to Dr. Young his master.

The fugitive slave presented the institution as having a degrading and negative effect on both black and white. Brown argues that by denying education to the slaves, the slaveholders kept their own children in ignorance.

Brown countered the pro-slavery claim that Negroes are morally inferior, inherently lazy and slothful with the charge that the human bondage inevitably degraded not only slave, but slaveholders and their sympathizers as well. He describes one of his slave masters as a "horse-race, cockfighter, gambler and withal an inveterate drunkard whose fits and anger would cause him to throw chairs at his servants and put them in the smoke house."

According to Brown's testimony, he was the private property of only three slaveholders, but he worked for seven different employers during the twenty years he was in captivity. The frequent change in employers and varied positions acquainted Brown with the many facets of slavery, and prepared him to speak and write from a broad and knowledgeable background.

His knowledge and exposure were not restricted to the United States. He tells of his travels in Europe where his itinerary took him more than twenty thousand miles lecturing on American slavery and pleading the cause of abolition. While Brown was abroad, he seized every opportunity to consolidate international public opinion against the institution of slavery. Brown's treatment of slavery transcends the provincial idiom.

Brown's consuming passion for freedom grew even more intense after the enactment of the Fugitive Slave Law. The Fugitive Slave Law was enacted while he was abroad, and his abolitionist position changed from "moral persuasion" to a "new militancy." He warned his audiences that if the moral struggle for freedom failed, a physical one would be inevitable.

Brown's commitment to the struggle for freedom for the blacks was a consuming passion that found expression through the idiom of literature. His novel, Clotel or The President's Daughter, revolves around a mulatto woman and her two beautiful daughters who are sold as slaves after the mother has been deserted by her white lover. The separate careers of the three women are traced, but the main character is Clotel, the President's daughter, who finally ends her tragic life by drowning in the Potomac River as she is pursued by slave catchers, who anticipated capturing her and returning her to the deep south.

The fact that Clotel dies in sight of the White House, occupied by Thomas Jefferson, is more than a coincidence, as the title of the novel suggests. Brown said that the tragedy of Clotel "should be an evidence wherever it should be known, of the unconquerable love of liberty the heart may inherit; as well as a fresh admonition to the slave dealer, of the cruelty and enormity of his crime." (47)

Brown consistently argued that the institution of slavery was a sad commentary on American society. He uses the novel to expose the evils of slavery and to refute the claims of the plantation tradition. The plantation tradition stereotyped the Negro as inherently inferior and happy only under supervision and protection of the white master on the plantation. (48)

Seventeen years after the Civil War, Brown published My Southern Home, or The South and Its People. In this, his final book, Brown shifted from simply describing the horrors and cruelties of slavery to analyzing and examining the race problems beyond abolition.

Brown observed that some of the most vocal abolitionists were paternalistic and discriminated against the people they were fighting to emancipate. Many abolitionists were incapable of proposing a program because they saw slavery as a moral abstraction and not as a social problem. Brown's constant contention and imaginative understanding of the problem which emancipation alone did not address outran the understanding of even so ardent an abolitionist as William Lloyd Garrison.

Brown, in contrast to many other abolitionists, maintained that the struggle for equality would be long and tedious, because the anti-slavery crusade succeeded in abolishing slavery but failed to alter the image of the Negro in the eyes of White America, or measurably improve the Negro's position in society.

Possibly, the most important message Brown ever delivered to blacks is the final sentence in My Southern Home: "Black men, don't be ashamed to show your colors and to own them!" Brown was aware of the fact that the Negro, as any American, must grapple with the universal "who am I?" However, unlike other ethnic groups, who brought their cultures, languages, and traditions with them to America, the Negro was virtually stripped of his past. Nevertheless, Brown saw as did DuBois, the eminent black scholar, that "there is nothing so indigenous, so completely 'made in America' as we [blacks]."

Brown's writings argue that American slavery was developed in such a way as to convince the whites that Negroes were inherently inferior and incapable of freedom. Equally important, the system of slavery was administered in a fashion to make the Negroes behave as if they were inferior--to distort their personalities and suppress their mentalities in such a way as to make them incapable of utilizing the "freedom" that finally became theirs after two-and-a-half centuries of enslavement. He attacked prejudice, not only because it was wrong, but because if accepted, it postponed the acceptance of the Negro and his establishment in his rightful place.

Understanding the peculiarity of slavery in America is the key to understanding both the white man's and black man's Negro problem. Tocqueville pointed out nearly a hundred and twenty-eight years ago that: "In the ancient world men could move from slavery to freedom without great difficulty because former slaves could not be distinguished from those who had always been free. The Negro by contrast, transmits the eternal mark of his ignominy to all his descendants; and although the law may abolish slavery, God alone can obliterate the trace of its existence." Although Brown, understandably, argued that "No people had borne oppression like the Negro, and no race had been so much imposed upon," he looked beyond the dimensions of the now toward the prospect of ultimate equality for the blacks.

Lacking some religiously oriented Moses to lead them, blacks came to freedom via political and military developments. Following emancipation, the American freedmen were left with the aftermath of war, terrors of the ex-slave-holders, the lies of carpet-baggers, and the contradictory advice of friends and foes. Undaunted by the complexity and difficulty of post-war life, Brown continued to offer analysis and understanding of the problem and to exhort the blacks with challenge and courage.

CHAPTER IX

CONCLUSION

The contention of the present work is that William Wells Brown wrote to correct impressions rather than to make them. Through a variety of experiences, he learned that the strongest obstacle to abolition and equal rights was the widespread belief, north and south, that the Negro race was naturally inferior. The theory of innate inferiority had been well formed and promoted by the pro-slavery apologists who expended much of their time and energy trying to prove that the persons of African descent were intellectually and socially inferior.

Brown's literary and historical writings appeared at a time when many Americans defended slavery on the grounds that Negroes were by nature shiftless, slovenly, childlike, dull-witted, savages, and incapable of assimilation as equals into a white society. The defenders of human bondage exhausted every possible resource to demonstrate that Negroes would only work under compulsion and were by nature barbarians and unable to take care of themselves.

Brown wrote and spoke for thirty years combating the stereotype of inherent inferiority of the Negro. It was his contention that the question of racial inferiority was integral to the whole slavery controversy, and that for three decades prior to the Civil War the slavery issue affected nearly every piece of national legislation. Brown believed that as long as the doctrine of racial inferiority prevailed, the abolitionists' cause would remain at a decided disadvantage. In light of this argument, Brown contered his attack against slavery on combating the popular notion of inherent racial inequality of the Negro.

First, Brown attacked the concept of racial inequality through his personal testimony, The Narrative. (49) In his popular autobiography of twenty years in human bondage, Brown gave an eyewitness account of how slaveholders and their sympathizers had employed every means imaginable to stamp a feeling of natural inferiority in the mind and soul of the Negro. Brown demonstrated through his personal testimony that slavery was designed to strip the Negro of his "sense of human worth" from the cradle to the grave.

Brown contended that slave owners (perhaps instinctively feeling that the inferiority which they attributed to blacks was not demonstrable) lost no opportunity to maintain a subservient attitude among the blacks and to destroy any self-confidence that remained in the enslaved people.

He recorded in his narrative that the institution of slavery denied him a name. During his boyhood, his slave master adopted a nephew whose name was also William. His master, Dr. Young, eliminated the confusion of having two Williams in the same household by changing Brown's first name from William to Sandford. The incident taught Brown the painful fact that a slave has nothing--not even a name. A slave had absolutely no rights which a white person was bound to respect. Brown noticed that even domesticated animals had a name, and he described his name changing as "the most cruel act that could be committed on my rights." (50)

His personal testimony exposed slavery as a dehumanizing and repulsive institution, where blacks were denied the right of knowing their age as well as their name. Ignorance of age allowed the slave trader to auction the slave at a higher price and also made it convenient to call him "boy" regardless of age. Brown recalled seeing his mother whipped severely by an overseer but he suppressed his natural inclination to defend his mother because he knew it was futile for a slave to challenge a white person, even in self-defense. His account of the notorious slave trader, Walker, taking a baby from a slave mother's arms and forcing her to leave her baby behind is chilling in its effect.

Brown cited instances of mothers having taken the lives of their children to preserve them from the hands of the slave traders, and of brothers having taken the lives of their sisters to protect their chastity.

Brown's Narrative points out that if the slaves' human qualities were left unchecked, the slaves would destroy the system. Slave owners feared taking their slaves through free states and exposing them to the company of free Negroes. Brown maintained, "that every slave community was in a volcano that was liable to burst out any moment." (51)

Brown's testimony indicates that slaves loved and cared for their families. He cited the incident of a despondent slave woman drowning herself over the thought of being forced to leave her husband. According to Brown's personal testimony, he refused to run away because he "could not bear the idea" of separation from his mother. He explained: "after she had undergone and suffered so much for me [I] would be proving recreant to the duty which I owe her." [sic] (52)

The Negro slaves' commitment and respect for family reveal that slaves were human beings with natural tendencies and aspirations as any other race of people. Brown's personal testimony repeatedly reveals that slavery was unnatural, unchristian, and indefensible.

His testimony suggests that slaveholders used religion to control their slaves and to augment the institution of slavery. Brown held that the religion offered the slaves was designed to keep them submissive and obedient rather than to save their souls. For example, the white preacher would sometimes ask slaves the questions to which they were expected to give the answers sympathetic to the compatibility of slavery and religion.

"Question: What command has God given to servants concerning obedience to their master?

Answer: Servants obey all things your master's according to the flesh, not with eye service as menpleasing, but in singleness of heart, fearing God.

Question: If a servant runs away, what should be done with him?

Answer: He should be caught and brought back.

Question: When he is brought back, what should be done with him?

Answer: Whip him well.

Question: Why may not the whites be slaves as well as the blacks?

Answer: Because the Lord intended the Negro for slaves.

Question: Are they better calculated for servants than the white?

Answer: Yes, their hands are large, the skin thick and tough, and they can stand the sun better than whites.

In reality, Brown dismissed the slaveholder's religion as a farce and its practitioners as mere hypocrites.

> Great damage was done the cause of Christianity by the position assumed on the question of slavery by the American churches, and especially those in the Southern states. Think of a religious kidnapper! A Christian slave-breeder! A slave-trader, loving his neighbor as himself, receiving the sacraments in some Protestant church from the hand of a Christian apostle, then the next day selling babies by the dozen, and tearing young women from the arms of their husbands to feed the lust of lecherous New Orleans! Imagine a religious man selling his own children into eternal bondage! Think of a Christian defending slavery out of the Bible, and declaring there is no higher law, but atheism is the first principle of Republic Government (53)

His testimony challenged the claim that slaves were innately shiftless and incapable of producing good work. He reported where one of his owners hired him out because he was a productive worker. The notorious slave trader, Walker, was so pleased with Brown's work that he paid his owner nine hundred dollars for a year's work. Brown recorded incidents in his writings in which slaveholders would borrow money from their slaves.

His autobiography added credibility to the abolitionist movement for it documented the case for freedom, and--by its very publication--attested to the ability of the Negro. His personal testimony underscored the dimension of ethical impact on the abolitionists' crusade for freedom.

William Lloyd Garrison could write convincingly and passionately about the separation of a slave from his mother, but Brown could give a personal testimony of watching the steamboat carrying his mother away forever. Wendell Phillips wrote about slaves who rebelled against the institution of human bondage, but Brown could give a first-hand account of Randall who was beaten unmercifully for speaking up for his rights. Theodore Weld could speak with passion about ugly wounds inflicted by slave drivers, but Brown could remove his shirt and produce the scars of such barbarism.

The ex-slave's autobiography was living indictment against the sleek, docile, content, dependent being presented in pro-slavery literature. The courageous and intelligent protest against slavery by an exslave, won the admiration and sympathy of many Americans. The following review was reported of the Brown Narrative in November 1855:

> The mere fact that the member of an outcast and enslaved race should accomplish his freedom and educate himself up to an equality of intellectual and moral vigor with the leaders of the race by which he was held in bondage, is in itself, so remarkable that the story of the change cannot be otherwise than exciting. For ourselves, we confess to have read it with the unbroken attention with which we absorbed Uncle Tom's Cabin. It has the advantage of the latter book in that it is no fiction. (54)

The sensitive and fair-minded reader of Brown's narrative would see that Negro slaves were human beings, with strengths and weaknesses like any other race of people.

Brown also countered the charge of inherent Negro inferiority on the grounds that the American tradition and ideal were incompatible with the institution of slavery. When we examine the influence of Slavery upon the character of the American people, we are led to believe that if the American Government ever had a character, she has lost it. I know that upon the 4th of July, our 4th of July orators talk of Liberty, Democracy, and Republicanism. They talk of liberty, while three million of their own countrymen are groaning in abject slavery. This is called the "land of the free, and the home of the brave"; it is called the "Asylum of the oppressed"; and some have been foolish enough to call it the "cradle of Liberty." If it is the "cradle of Liberty," they have rocked the child to death. American history records that the blood of black men as well as white men was spilled so that America might be free. Therefore, it is contended that Black and White were entitled to the freedom they fought for and won in the Revolutionary War and were promised in the declarations and other documents for freedom. In his writings, Brown commemorated the blacks who fought and died to maintain the freedom of the nation. Brown contended that the institution of slavery was a contradiction of the natural rights philosophy and the Declaration of Independence.

He argued that the doctrine of Negro inferiority, which buttressed slavery, was embedded in the laws and sanctioned by the white population both north and south. Brown charged the United States Constitution with condoning and protecting the peculiar institution. The Constitution does not mention slavery by name and does not overtly support human bondage, but in giving slavery certain indirect protection (the three-fifth clause, non-interference for 21 years with the slave trade, the fugitive slave proviso), the Constitution seemed to sanction slavery.

> I would have the constitution torn in shreds and scattered to the four winds of heaven. Let us destroy the constitution, and build on its ruins the temple of liberty. I have brothers and sisters in slavery. I have seen chains placed on their limbs and beheld them carried captive. We have nothing to do with the consequence of the dissolution of the union. Let us do what is right and let the consequences take care of themselves. When the patriots of the revolution struck the blow for liberty, they did not ask wl t would be the consequences. (55)

Brown was one of the first black writers to use history to vindicate the character of the Negro from the popular belief of inherent inferiority. The Black Man, His Antecedents, His Genius, and His Achievements, published in 1863, was written for the express purpose of combating the popular notion of the inherent inferiority of the Negro and to help mobilize support for Lincoln's emancipation policy. The abolitionists heralded Brown's publication as "just the book for the hour," and Lewis Tappan, a prominent merchant and philanthropist, said, "it will do more for the colored man's elevation than any work yet published." Frederick Douglass called Brown's book "an additional installation of the black man's reply to the damaging charge of natural and permanent inferiority."

Brown sought to redeem the character and ancestry of the Negro by contending that which is the general opinion of many historians and ethnologists, that the Ethiopians were really Negroes, and the American Negro is their descendant. According to this theory, Ethiopians are regarded as the earliest race to attain a high degree of civilization. Brown argued that their accomplishments, which are inscribed upon monuments extending from India to Ethiopia, cannot be obliterated from the pages of history.

He admitted that the present state of Negroes would not compare favorably to the white race, but explained the circumstances with reference to two-and-a-half centuries of enslavement and a government which had sanctioned acceptance of the theory for natural inferiority of the Negro.

History contends that there was a time when the blacks stood at the head of science and literary contributions, while the Anglo-Saxons were a "rude and barbarous people, divided into numerous tribes, dressed in skins of wild beasts."

Brown raised the rhetorical question, "from whence sprang the Anglo-Saxon? For, mark you, it is he that denies the equality of the Negro....When the Romans invaded Britain, they reduced the people to a state of vassalage as degrading as that of slavery in the southern states." Sarcastically, Brown chided, "this is not very flattering to the President's ancestors, but it is just....I am sorry that Mr. Lincoln came from such a low origin, but he is not to blame. I only find fault with him for making mouth at me..." (56)

Brown contended there was no need for despair because the Negro has the intellectual genius which God has given him, which needs, only, an opportunity to fulfill its potentials. History records no account of a nation, which, by its own unaided efforts, or by some powerful inward impulse, has risen from barbarism to civilization and respectability.

Brown observed there is nothing in race or blood, in color or features, that imparts susceptibility of improvement to one race over another. The mind left to itself from infancy, without culture, remains a blank. Knowledge is not innate. Development makes man. As the Greeks, the Romans, and Jews drew knowledge from the Egyptians three thousand years ago, and the Europeans received it from the Romans, so must blacks of this land rise in the same way.

Brown maintained that historically those who have opposed abolition have argued that the two races cannot live together in a state of freedom. Thirty years before Brown, it was argued in England that "if you liberate the slaves of the West Indies, they can't live

with the whites in a state of freedom." The facts of
the matter reveal the contrary. The blacks and whites
live together in Jamaica; they are all prosperous, and
the island is in a better condition than it was before
the act of emancipation was passed.

In his response to the charge of inherent inferiority with reference to history, Brown pointed out that
the majority of the Blacks in the northern American
states were descended from slaves and many of them were
slaves themselves. In defiance of racial prejudice,
he considered that educational, moral, and industrial
development of free blacks in the north compared favorably with that of any laboring class in the world.
Considering the fact that blacks are shut out of many
trades and professions, Brown observed that it is
marvelous that blacks have attained the position they
now occupy. Notwithstanding these bars, young blacks
have learned trades, become artists, gone into the
professions, although bitter prejudice may prevent them
from having a great deal of practice. When it is considered that they have mostly come out of bondage, and
that their calling has been the lowest kind in every
community, it is still strange that the colored people
have amassed so much wealth in every state in the Union.
If this is not an exhibition of capacity, declared
Brown, "I don't understand the meaning of the term."
(57)

The history of Negro slaves on the plantation in
the south suggests that the Negroes have character and
ability to achieve like any other race. Brown contended
that the enslaved of the south are as capable of self-
support as any other class of people in the country.
He testified that a large class of slaves have been
for years accustomed to hire their time from their
owners. Some able mechanics have been known to pay as
high as six hundred dollars per annum, beside providing themselves with food and clothing; and this class
of slaves, by their industry, have taken care of themselves so well, and their appearance has been so respectable, that many of the states have passed laws
prohibiting masters from letting their slaves out to
themselves, because as it was said, it made the other
slaves dissatisfied to see so many of their fellows
well provided for, and accumulating something for
themselves in the way of pocket money.

Brown raised a rhetorical question, "What shall we
do with the slave of the south?" His answer [was to]:

"Expatriate him because he cleared up the swamps, he has built up towns, cities and villages; he has enriched the north and Europe with his cotton, and sugar, and rice; and for this you would drive him out the country!"

Brown argued that those who raised the question, "What shall be done with the slaves if they are freed" would be better off asking, "What shall we do with the slaveholders if the slaves are freed?" Brown contended that "the slave has shown himself better fitted to take care of himself than the slaveholder. He has the sinew, the determination, and the will; and if you will take the free colored people of the south as the criterion, take their past history as a sample of what the colored people are capable of doing, every one must be satisfied that the slaves can take care of themselves." (58)

In brief, Brown contended that the institution of slavery encouraged indolence among slaves and robbed them of their initiative and motivation. Given liberty and a fair wage, contended Brown, blacks would become more productive and enhance the southern economy. Instead of abolition destroying the economy of the south, it would strengthen the economy by making the Negro a consumer, and increase the demand for more manufactured goods in the north. His historical deliberation shows that blacks are human with intelligence and character like other people, and the facts refute that they are innately inferior.

Brown continued his assault against the popular notion of the natural inferiority of the Negro by quoting the Bible to prove the equality and unity of the human race. He cited the Genesis account of the creation which indicates that all men are created in the image of God. Brown quoted [where] Paul's admonition to the people of Athens, "that God hath made of one blood all nations of men for to dwell on the face of the earth." Acts 17:26. The scripture sanctioned Brown's contention that skin color does not alter the unity of the human race.

Brown challenged a popular pro-slavery argument that color originated with the curse of Cain.

> For if Cain was the progenitor of Noah, and if Cain's new peculiarities were perpetuated, then as Noah was the father of the world's new population the question would be, not how to account for any of the human family being black, but how can we account for any

being white. (59)

Brown passionately believed that the assumption of innate inferiority of the Negro was the chief cornerstone bolstering the institution of slavery. Even after the Civil War, the belief of Negro inferiority underlaid most of the arguments against granting the freed[men] equal opportunities in education, voting and civil rights.

Brown insisted that the adverse environmental effects of slavery and discrimination, rather than natural deficiencies, were responsible for the inadequacies of the Negro in American society. He charged that it was unrealistic to expect a people who had suffered more than two centuries of slavery to attain social equality immediately. Brown accused the pro-slavery sympathizers with confusing freedom with social equality. "I have some white neighbors around me in Cambridge," he writes, "who are not very intellectual; they don't associate with my family; but whenever they shall improve themselves, and bring themselves up by their own intellectual and moral worth, I shall not object to their coming into my society--all things being equal" He recognized that blacks must earn social equality, but Brown contended that the first step is for the "white man to take his heels off our necks, and let us have a chance to rise by our own efforts." (60.)

Brown insisted that two-and-a-half centuries of slavery were responsible for the Negroes' debilitating condition rather than innate inferiority. Slavery was designed to make the Negro appear stupid, helpless, and childlike. The scars slavery left on the intellectual, industrial and moral development could not be healed overnight. "What stone has been left unturned to degrade us?" asked James M'Cune Smith, a leading Negro abolitionist of New York City, in 1860. What hand has refused to fan the flame of popular prejudice against us?....What press has not ridiculed and condemned us? No other nation on the globe could have made more progress in the midst of such universal and stringent disparagement. It would humble the proudest, crush the energies of the strongest, and retard the progress of the swiftest."

Brown argued that the Negro had the latent potential to be equal with whites, but it would take time for the manifestation of his innate ability. He reminded the opponents to freedom that "men going from slavery to freedom cannot change their habits as they change their garments."

Brown insisted that inherent immorality and dishonesty attributed to the Negro is the product of degenerate environment created by the institution of slavery. Under the tutelage of slavery promiscuity was encouraged, marriage had no legal validity, and the father had no personal responsibility for his children, who belonged not to their parents, but their master. "A slave is one that is in the power of an owner. He is a chattel; he is a thing; he is a piece of property. A master can dispose of him, can dispose of his labor, can dispose of his wife, can dispose of his offspring, can dispose of everything that belongs to the slave, and the slave shall have no right to speak; he can have nothing to say. The slave cannot speak for himself; he cannot speak for his wife, or his children. For instance, Brown's mother had seven children and no two of them had the same father. He made the following statement about his father: "My father's name, as I learned from my mother was George Higgins. He was a white man, a relative of my master, and connected with some of the first families in Kentucky."

Brown told the Female Anti-Slavery Society of Salem, Massachusetts on November 14, 1847 that slavery had a profound and pervasive influence on the morals of society in general.

> Go into the slaveholding states, and there you can see the master going into the church, on the Sabbath, with his slave following him into the church, and waiting upon him--both belonging to the same church. And the day following, the master puts his slave upon the auction-stand, and sells him to the highest bidder. The church does not condemn him; the law does not condemn him; but the slaveholder walks through the community after he has sold a brother belonging to the same church with himself, as if he had not committed an offense against God. (61)

The residue of slavery not only had a negative effect on the Negro but on the larger community as well. He observed that, "No man can bind a change around the limb of his neighbor, without the inevitable fate of fastening the other end around his own body." There was a mutual network of interdependence between the slaves and the slaveholders. While the slave masters degraded their slaves, they themselves were debased.

By preventing education from reaching the slaves, the slaveholders kept their own children in ignorance. There is some truth in the adage which says, "It is hard to keep a dog in a ditch without getting dirty and staying in the ditch yourself."

The demoralization which the institution enacted upon all classes in the community in which it existed was indeed fearful to contemplate; and we may well say that slavery is the curse of curses. While it made the victim a mere chattel, taking from him every characteristic of manhood, it degraded the mind of the master, brutalized his feelings, seared his conscience, and destroyed his moral sense.

Brown countered the pro-slavery argument that the Negro was by nature sweet, docile, happy, childlike and satisfied with his slave status, by contending that many slaves who deport themselves in a docile manner do so as a survival tactic in a hostile society. The cruelties of the peculiar institution had taught the slaves that any sign of resistance would be futile in a slave community. Glen, one of the leading characters in Brown's play, <u>The Escape or Leap for Freedom</u>, spoke the sentiment of some slaves when he said, "There is a volcano pent up in the hearts of slaves of these southern states that will burst forth ere long. I would be willing to die, if I could smite down with these chains every man who attempts to enslave his fellow man." Negro slaves were adept at pleasing their slaveholders while despising them. In his drama, Brown portrayed Cato as a loyal and happy-go-lucky slave but when the opportunity presented itself, he escaped from slavery. It is true that some slaves would scratch where it did not itch and would laugh when it was not funny, but these gestures were survival mechanisms rather than innate characteristics.

During the decade of the 1850s, Brown grew more and more pessimistic over the prospects of freedom and Negro equality. The Fugitive Slave Act, the resurgence of the American Colonization Society, the unsuccessful attempts to win suffrage, and the Dred Scott decision underscored the facts that whites were determined to maintain their position of racial superiority.

Brown saw that the theory of inherent inferiority of the Negro had had a pervasive influence on the total American society. Even the Anti-Slavery Society was not given a clean bill of health from racial prejudice.

In spite of the fact that the Anti-Slavery Society denounced racial prejudice and embraced the blacks' claim for full citizenship, white abolitionists were divided on the question of social equality for their black members. Brown resented the fact that blacks were frequently treated as second class citizens in the Anti-Slavery Society. He was annoyed by the patronizing attitude of some white abolitionists, and the application of a double standard which sanctioned the pro-slavery argument of black inferiority. Even the celebrated abolitionist William Lloyd Garrison commented that the Negroes' high visibility made him an object of prejudice.

> The black color of the body, the wooly hair, the thick lips...forms so striking a contrast to the caucasian race that they may be distinguished at a glance. They are branded by the hand of nature with a perpetual mark of disgrace. (62)

Brown charged some abolitionists with promoting the stereotypes of the Negro being innately meek, servile, comical, minstrel-like beings. For instance, William Ellery Channing described the Negro as "among the mildest, gentlest of men; and more open to religious impressions than the white man. (Channing meant that the Negro race is innately more gullible, naive and simple than the white race.)...if civilized, the African would undoubtedly show less energy, courage, and intellectual originality than the caucasian but would surpass him in amiableness, tranquility, gentleness, and content; he might never equal the white man 'in outward condition,' but he would probably be 'a much happier race'." (63) With this attitude, it was easy for the abolitionist to contend that social equality with blacks was not only impolite but unnatural.

There were abolitionists who worked for the Negroes' freedom but refused to crusade for his equality and citizenship. Brown noted that Emancipation Proclamation marked an end to slavery but not the race problem. The emancipation freed the slave but ignored the Negro. Brown noted that President Lincoln promised in his inaugural address that the Civil War would not change the status of the Negro in the rebel states and he committed himself against any interference with the condition of the blacks. "If a man has no vote for the men and the measures which tax himself, his family, and his property, and all which determines his reputation, that man is still a slave," argued Brown.

The stigma of Negro inferiority had touched nearly every segment of American society. Alexis de Tocqueville commenting on the race problem said: "In those parts of the union which the Negroes are no longer slaves they have no wise drawn nearer to the whites. On the contrary, the prejudice of race appears to be stronger in states that have abolished slavery than in those where it still existed; and nowhere is it so intolerant as in those states where servitude has never been known." (64) Racial prejudice in the north, the double-standards which existed in the anti-slavery society, and a lack of commitment to Negro equality strengthened the pro-slavery position that the Negro by accident of birth is an inferior race. With the prevailing racial attitude north and south, Brown was cognizant of the fact that the struggle for freedom would not be easy, because the anti-slavery crusade had not altered the image of the Negro in the eyes of White America, nor measurably improved the Negroes' position. Brown wrote that one of the bitterest fruits of slavery in our land is the cruel spirit of caste, which makes the complexion even of the free Negro a badge of social inferiority, exposing him to insults in the steamboat and railcar, and in all places of public resort, not even excepting the church; banishing him from remunerative occupation; expelling him from the legislative hall, the magistrates' bench, and the jury box; and crushing his noblest aspiration under a weight of prejudice and proscription which he struggles in vain to throw off.

Even after the Emancipation, Brown feared that the Negroes' condition would be worse than that of slavery and the prospect of reenslavement was a strong possibility. If human bondage was reinstated, Brown said, "he would go down south, and help accomplish the good works of bearing arms against the south."

Following the Civil War, Brown continued to crusade for social equality for Blacks. Repeatedly, argued that freedom should not be confused with social equality, and that the Negro must earn respect. Brown wrote: "To gain the social prize, paddle your own canoe." Given the chance, blacks have the ability to earn social equality. Brown cited examples in the south where black social and educational status surpassed that of many whites. In many ways, the institution of slavery had equipped the ex-slaves with more culture and job skills than their white counterpart. Brown argued that whites were more afraid of the Negroes' ability and industry than of his color rubbing off against them.

In short, after the Emancipation, the popular notions that God had made the black man to perform menial tasks and that, accordingly, he should be barred from "respectable" jobs still prevailed. With the notion of black inferiority so deeply entrenched in the fabric of American society, it was natural that Brown should direct much and frequent attention to the necessity for social equality, if the free blacks were to realize their potential. Brown's persistent contention that abolition extended beyond "legal" freedom distinguished him from many of his contemporary freedom fighters.

NOTES

Chapter I   Sandford's Lot

(1) Josephine Brown, <u>Biography of an American Bondman by His Daughter</u>. (Boston, 1856), pp. 10-11.
<u>Narrative of William W. Brown. A Fugitive Slave. Written by himself</u>, p. 13. Boston, Anti-Slavery Office, 1848. See Lerone Bennett, Jr. <u>Before the Mayflower: A History of Black America</u>. (Chicago: Johnson Publishing Co.) 1969, 137-38, 258, and <u>Anti-Slavery Bugle</u>, May 5, 1855.

William Edward Farrison, <u>William Wells Brown Author and Reformer</u>. (Chicago: University Press, 1969).

<u>Narrative of the Life of Frederick Douglass, An American Slave</u>. Boston, 1845, pp. 1-2. See John Herbert Nelson, <u>The Negro Character in American Literature</u>. (Lawrence, Kansas: Department of Journalism Press, 1926).

Narrative of William Wells Brown, op. cit., pp. 95-96. See Francis Pendleton Gaines, <u>The Southern Plantation: A Study in the Development and Accuracy of a Tradition</u>. (New York: Columbia University Press, 1921).

Carter G. Woodson, <u>The Negro Professional Man and the Community, with Special Emphasis on the Physician and the Lawyer</u> (Washington, D.C.: Association for the Study of Negro Life and History, 1935).

John W. Blassingame, <u>The Slave Community</u>.(New York: Oxford University Press, 1972), pp. 158-159. See Harold Charles Nichols, <u>Many Thousand Gone: The Ex-Slaves' Account of their Bondage and Freedom</u>. (Leiden, Netherlands: E.J. Brill, 1963).

See Fay David, ed. "Introduction," in <u>Black Defiance: Black Profiles in Courage</u>. (New York: William Morrow and Co.), 1972, pp. 34-35.

William Wells Brown, <u>The Black Man</u>, (Boston: R.F. Wallcut, 221 Washington St., 1863).

Dred Scott was the slave of John Emerson who resided in the pro-slave state of Missouri. In 1834 Scott moved with his master to Illinois and then to the territory of Wisconsin, which prohibited slavery. In 1838, Scott and his master returned to Missouri, where Emerson died in 1843. Scott sued his master's widow for freedom on the grounds that his former residence in a free state and free territory made him a free man. The case went to Supreme Court of the United States where Chief Justice Roger B. Taney pronounced in 1857 that no Negro--free or slave--could (continued) claim United States citizenship and that Congress could not prohibit slavery in the United States territories.

Narrative of William Wells Brown, pp. 39-40, 64. See Harrison Anthony Trexler, Slavery in Missouri, 1804-1865. Johns Hopkins University Studies in Historical and Political Science, No. 32. Baltimore: Johns Hopkins Press, 1918.

"William Wells Brown, Social Reformer," Journal of Negro History 39 (1954).

Ibid., p. 26. See William Hyde, Encyclopaedia of the History of St. Louis, 1899, III, 1313., and Henry Tanner, History of the Rise and Progress of Alton Riots, 1878.

See Robert Starobin, Industrial Slavery in the Old South. New York: Oxford University Press, 1970.

(2) Narrative of William Wells Brown, pp. 28-29.

Chapter II A Strange and Cruel Democracy

(3) Ibid., pp. 82-83. See Anthony Harrison Trexler, Slavery in Missouri 1804-1865. Johns Hopkins University Studies in Historical and Political Science, No. 32. Baltimore: Johns Hopkins Press, 1918, pp. 183-260.

(4) William Wells Brown, Black Man, p. 17.

See Charles H. Nichols, ed., Black Men in Chains: Narratives by Escaped Slaves. New York: Lawrence Hill and Co., 1972.

See Stephen T. Butterfield, "The Use of Language in the Slave Narratives." Negro American Literature Forum, 6 (Fall), 1972.

See Jean Fagan Yellin. The Intricate Knot: Black Figures in American Literature, 1776-1863. New York University Press, 1972.

Richard Randolph, "Social Origins of Distinguished Negroes, 1770-1865." Journal of Negro History, 40, July 1955.

See William Edward Farrison, "A Flight Across Ohio: The Escape of William Wells Brown from Slavery." Ohio State Archaeological and Historical Quarterly, 61, July 1952.

Chapter III William Wells

(5) See "Letter from W. W. Brown," *National Anti-Slavery Standard*, April 21, 1855, p. 3.
The Narrative of William Wells Brown, p. 96.

Chapter IV Freedom

(6) William Wells Brown, *The American Fugitive in Europe. Sketches of Places and People Abroad* (Boston: J. F. Jewett and Co.), pp. 34-35. Also see Josephine Brown, *Biography of an American Bondman* (Boston: R. F. Wallcut, 1856), p. 95. and *North Star* (August 3, 1849), p. 3.
William Wells Brown, *Sketches of Places and People Abroad*, p. 39.
William Wells Brown, *Three Years in Europe* (London: C. Gilpin, 1852), pp. 6-8.

(7) Ibid., p. 54.
Ibid., p. 35.
Ibid., p. 50. See Maria W. Chapman, "Letter From Maria W. Chapman," *Liberator*, September 28, 1849, p. 156. M. Alexis de Tocqueville (1805-1859), French historian and politician, was one of the most perceptive observers during the 19th century of the tendencies of political and social democracy. He spent a year (1831-32) in the United States studying American penal system and the democratic society. In most of his writings he was concerned with one basic problem: the evolution of democratic society. In one of his most popular books, *Democracy in America,* he sought to show how equalitarian attitudes and popular government had affected the social system in America. He considered the disappearance of rigid class division as the most striking feature of the new society.
George Thompson (1804-1878), an antislavery advocate, born at Liverpool on June 11, 1804, was widely known for his abolitionist activities against slavery in the British colonies. A series of lectures by him led to the formation of the Edinburgh Society for the Abolition of Slavery throughout the World. He was acquainted with William Lloyd Garrison and visited the United States on several occasions in support of abolition in this country. See "American Slavery: Meeting to Welcome the Fugitive Slave, Mr. William Wells Brown," *Liberator*, September 28, 1849, p. 154; *North Star*, October 5, 1849, p. 2; and George Thompson, "Letter from George Thompson," *Liberator*, September 21, 1849, p. 150.

(8) Toussaint L'Ouverture (1743-1803), a Haitian soldier, statesman and martyr, in 1791, led a slave revolt against France. In 1793 the National Convention in France proclaimed freedom for the slaves. He fought in the French Army against the Spanish and the British.

In 1799, a civil war erupted between the Negroes and the mulattoes. Toussaint, as leader of the full-blooded Negroes, soon found himself the ruler of the island. Haiti enjoyed prosperity under his reign. In 1802, Napoleon decided to reestablish slavery in Haiti. Toussaint led the resistance against slavery. He was captured and taken to France where he died as a prisoner. See William Wells Brown, Rising Son, pp. 145-172 and Wilson Armistaed, Tribute for the Negro (London: Charles Gilpin, 1848).

(9) "St. Domingo: Its Revolutions and its Patriots," published in 1855, p. 37. This speech and "A Lecture Delivered Before the Female Anti-Slavery Society of Salem," published in 1847, were apparently the only two printed as pamphlets. However, excerpts from Brown's speeches appeared in the abolitionist newspapers. See National Anti-Slavery Standard, June 6, 1857, p. 2; Liberator, June 5, 1857. p. 89; and Howard H. Bell, "National Negro Conventions of the Middle 1840s: Moral Suasion vs. Political Action." Journal of Negro History 42 (October 1957): 247-60.

(10) William Wells Brown, Three Years in Europe, p. 249.

William Wells Brown, The Black Man: His Antecedent, His Genius, and His Achievements (Boston: Thomas Hamilton, 1863), p. 6. See Carter G. Woodson and Charles H. Wesley, Negro Makers of History (Washington, D.C.: Associated Publishers, 1928), pp. 176-77, 202.

(11) William Wells Brown, The Black Man, p. 32. See Wilson Armistead, A Tribute for the Negro, pp. 52, 120-43.

William Wells Brown, The Black Man, p. 33.

(12) Ibid., pp. 35-36. See Liberator, June 13, 1862, p. 96.

Chapter V   The Call to Battle

(13) Samuel Ringgold Ward, *The Autobiography of a Fugitive Negro* (New York: Arno Press, 1968), p. 32.

(14) William Wells Brown, *The Rising Son*, p.270. Armistead, *A Tribute for the Negro*, pp. 252-55.
Frank Tannenbaum, *Slave and Citizen* (New York: Alfred A. Knopf, 1947, pp. 106-07.

(15) Ibid., p. 277.

(16) William Lloyd Garrison, *Thoughts on African Colonization or An Impartial Exhibition Doctrine, Principles and Purpose of the American Colonization Society* (Boston: Garrison and Knapp, 1832), pp. 40-41.

(17) Ibid., p. 337. See Eugene D. Genovese, *Roll, Jordan, Roll* (New York: Pantheon Books, 1974), pp. 188-94.
William Wells Brown, *The Rising Son*, p. 337.

(18) William Wells Brown, *The Negro in the American Rebellion*, p. 39.

(19) Speech at Cooper Union, February 12, 1862, Report in *New York Tribune,* February 13, 1862. See *Liberator*. August 15, 1862, p. 135. Brown noted that there is no need for slave insurrection, because white men are killing each other off. Brown urged the Union government to declare emancipation and that would cause former slaves to fight for their freedom.

(20) William Wells Brown, *The Negro in the American Rebellion*, p. 127. See Wendell Phillips Garrison and Francis Jackson Garrison, *William Lloyd Garrison 1805-1897: The Story of His Life Told by His Children* (New York: Century Co.) vol. 4, p. 79.

(21) Ibid., pp. 143-44.

(22) Ibid., p. 162. See McPherson, *The Negro's Civil War*, pp. 164-68. Thomas Wentworth Higginson (1823-1911), a reformer soldier, author, was born in Cambridge, Massachusetts. At an early age he entered Harvard and graduated with honors. He taught school but his two favorite causes were women's suffrage and opposition to slavery. In 1851 he was called to Boston to join a vigilance committee for the rescue of a fugitive slave. Three years later he was summoned to

(continued) take part in the liberation of another fugitive slave, Anthony Burns, about to be returned from Boston to his owner in the south. Unlike many of the leading anti-slavery reformers, who refused on principle to advocate violence, Higginson had no reservations about the use of force in combatting slavery. Higginson found it natural soon after the outbreak of the Civil War to stop his preaching and prepare for fighting. In 1862 he was offered and accepted command of the first Negro regiment in the Union Army. Higginson held command of the First South Carolina Volunteers from November 1862 until May 1864. His experiences with the black soldiers in camp at Beaufort, South Caolina, and on skirmishing and raiding expeditions up the St. Mary's and South Edisto Rivers afforded abundant material for his book, Army Life in a Black Regiment (1870). (See Mary Thacker Higginson, Thomas Wentworth Higginson: The Stor of His Life (1914) and Journals of Thomas Wentworth Higginson (1921).

(23) William Wells Brown, The Negro in the American Rebellion, p. 225.

(24) Ibid. See Kenneth M. Stamp, The Era of Reconstruction 1865-1877 (New York: Vintage Books, 1965), pp. 51-82.

(25) William Wells Brown, The Negro in the American Rebellion, p. 335.

(26) Ibid., pp. 339-40.

(27) Ibid., p. 341. See Dubois, The Era of Reconstruction, pp. 122-23.

Chapter VI A Mighty Pen

(28) William Wells Brown, Clotel, or, The President's Daughter: A Narrative of Slave Life in the United States. (London: Partridge and Oakey, 1853), Preface.
Noel Hermance. William Wells Brown and Clotel: A Portrait of the Artist in the First Negro Novel. (Archon Book, 1969), Preface VII-VIII. See "New York by W. W. Brown." Liberator, Feb. 3, 1854, p. 191.

William Wells Brown, Clotelle: A Tale of the Southern States. (Boston and New York, 1864), p. 104. See Herbert Ross Brown, The Sentimental Novel in America, 1789-1860. (Durham, North Carolina: Duke University Press, 1940), pp. 278-79.

(29) Ibid., pp. 66-67. See Sterling Brown, The Negro in American Fiction. (Washington, D.C.: The Associates in Negro Folk Education, 1937), p. 63.
Ibid., pp. 63-64. The rumor about Jefferson's slave mistress was bandied about by some of the abolitionists. See Levi Gaylord, "A Scene at New Orleans," Liberator, September 21, 1838. See The Liberator, February 3, 1854. Early political enemies of Jefferson had not ignored the scandal. See William Cullen Bryant, "The Embargo or, Sketches of the Times," 1808.

(30) See Buron Edward Reuter, The Mulatto in the United States, (Boston: Richard G. Badger, 1918), p. 65.

(31) Ibid., p. 84. See Bernard N. Bell, "Literary Sources of the Early Afro-American Novel," College Language Association Journal (18 September, 1974), p. 85.

Chapter VII High Propaganda

(32) Ibid. See Lorenzo Dow Turner, Anti-Slavery Sentiment in American Literature Prior to 1865. (Washington, D.C.: Association For the Study of Negro Life and History, 1929), pp. 79-81, 83-84, 104.

(33) William Wells Brown, The Escape, Or, A Leap for Freedom, p. 11.

(34) Ibid.

(35). Ibid., p. 33.
Ibid., p. 33. See Henry C. Wright, "William Wells Brown--His Dramas--Their Power for Good." Liberator, October 8, 1858, p. 163.

(36) Ibid., p. 35.
Ibid., p. 31.

(37) Ibid., pp. 38-39.

(38) Ibid., p. 8.

(39) Ibid., p. 44.

(40) William Wells Brown, My Southern Home, New Jersey: The Gregg Press, 1880, p. 164.

(41) See National Anti-Slavery Standard, January 10, 1863, p. 180.
See also DuBois, W.E.B., Black Reconstruction in America. An essay toward a history of the past which Black folk played in the attempt to reconstruct democracy in America, 1860-1880. Atheneum, 1962, p. 713. His comments and assessment of the importance the Negroes played in Reconstruction are similar to those made by Dr. DuBois in Black Reconstruction: "White historians have ascribed the faults and failures of Reconstruction to Negro ignorance and corruption. But the Negro insists that it was Negro loyalty and Negro vote alone that restored the south to the Union; established the new democracy, both for white and black, and instituted the public school." p. 713.

(42) William Wells Brown, My Southern Home, p. 234.

(43) Ibid.

(44) Ibid., p. 247.

(45) Ibid., p. 216. On Brown's return from Europe, he was quoted as saying, "Our own education and elevation is to be one of the main levers to overthrow the institution of slavery in these United States." See Provincial Freeman, November 11, 1854, pp. 1-2.

(46) William Wells Brown, My Southern Home, p. 233. See August Meier, Negro Thought in America, 1880-1915. Ann Arbor: University of Michigan Press, 1963, p. 233.

Chapter VIII   The Color of Ham and Cain

(47) William Wells Brown, Clotel; or, The President's Daughter. A Narrative of Slave Life in the United States. (London: Partridge and Oakey, 1853), p. 177

(48) Sterling Brown defines the plantation tradition in the following manner: "The pattern seldom varied: scenes of bliss on the plantation alternated with scenes of squalor in the free North. The contented slave, the down and the wretched freedman are the Negro stereotype....A plantation with a kindly master was basis for generalizing about all plantations, of whatever type, in whatever sections. A pampered houseservant, who refuses uncertain freedom for a comparative easy place, becomes the Negro slave; a poor unemployed wretch becomes the freedman. Miscegenation is missing in spite of the proofs walking about in great houses or the fields or the slave pens. Slavery is shown as a beneficent guardianship, never as a system of cheap and abundant labor that furnished the basis of a few large fortunes (and assured an impoverished, disfranchised class of poor whites)." Sterling Brown, The Negro in American Fiction (New York: Atheneum, 1969), p. 28.

Chapter IX Conclusion

(49) The slave narratives marked the beginning of a tradition of protest in Negro writings. The narratives played a vital role in changing the attitude of Americans toward Negroes. Within two years, eight thousand copies of Brown's Narrative had been sold. See Charles Nichols, "Who Read the Slave Narrative?" Phylon (Second Quarter), 1959, pp. 49-50. See Narrative of W.W. Brown, a fugitive Slave, written by himself. Liberator, September 3, 1847, p. 141 and William S. Braithwaite, "Alain Locke's Relationship to the Negro in American Literature." Phylon, 18 (Second Quarter), 1957, pp. 166-73.

(50) The Narrative of William Wells Brown, p. 97.

(51) William Wells Brown, The Black Man: His Antecedent, His Genius, and His Achievements. (Boston: Thomas Hamilton, 1863), p. 73.

(52) The Narrative of William Wells Brown, pp. 31-32.

(53) William Wells Brown, The Negro in the American Rebellion. (Boston: A. G. Brown and Co., 28 East Canton Street, 1880), pp. 38-39.

(54) Putnam's Monthly, VI, No. 35. November 1855, p. 547.

(55) <u>National Anti-Slavery Standard</u>, May 16, 1844, pp. 198-199. See also <u>Liberator</u>, May 18, 1855, pp. 78-79.

(56) <u>National Anti-Slavery Standard</u>, August 1, 1863, p. 33.

(57) Ibid., p. 40-41.

(58) Ibid., p. 46.

(59) William Wells Brown, <u>Rising Son,</u> pp. 46-47. See "Can the Slaveholder Be a Christian?" <u>Liberator</u>, August 10, 1849, p. 127.

(60) William Wells Brown, <u>The Black Man</u>, p. 29.

(61) William Wells Brown, "A Lecture Delivered Before the Female Anti-Slavery Society of Salem, At Lyceum Hall," November 14, 1847. Boston, Mass. Anti-Slavery Society No. 21, Cornhill 1847, p. 10.

(62) <u>The Liberator</u>, January 22, 1831.

(63) William Ellery Channing. "The African Character," in John A. Collins (ed.) The <u>Anti-Slavery Pickneck</u> (Boston, 1842).

(64) Alexis de Tocqueville, <u>Democracy in America,</u> ed. Phillips Bradley (2 Vol., New York, 1945), p. 1, 373. See "Sketches of the Sayings and Doings at the N. E. Anti-Slavery Convention." <u>Liberator</u>, June 4, 1847, p. 91.

BIBLIOGRAPHY

Primary Sources

Brown, William Wells. "A Lecture Delivered Before the Female Anti-Slavery Society of Salem" at Lyceum Hall, November 14, 1847.

_____. Narrative of William W. Brown, a Fugitive Slave. Boston, The Anti-Slavery Office. 1847.

_____. Three Years in Europe; or, Places I Have Seen and People I Have Met. With a memoir of the Author, by William Farmer. London: C. Gilpin, 1852.

_____. Clotel; or, The President's Daughter. A Narrative of Slave Life in the United States. London: Partridge and Oakey, 1853.

_____. The American Fugitive in Europe. Sketches of Places and People Abroad. With a memoir of the Author. Boston: J.P. Jewett and Company, 1855.

_____. St. Domingo: Its Revolutions and Its Patriots. A Lecture, Delivered Before the Metropolitan Athenaeum, London, May 16, 1855 and at St. Thomas' Church, Philadelphia, December 20, 1854. Boston: Bela Marsh.

_____. The Escape: or, A Leap for Freedom. A Drama in Five Acts. Boston: R.F. Wallcut, 1858.

_____. The Black Man: His Antecedents, His Genius, and His Achievements. Boston: R. F. Wallcut, 1863.

_____. Clotelle: A Tale of the Southern States. Boston: James Redpath and Company, 1864.

_____. Clotelle; or, The Colored Heroine. A Tale of the Southern States. Boston: Lee and Shepard, 1867.

_____. The Negro in the American Rebellion, His Heroism and His Fidelity. Boston: Lee and Shepard, 1867.

Brown, William Wells. *The Rising Son; or, The Antecedents and Advancement of the Colored Race.* Boston: A. G. Brown and Co., 1874.

_____. *My Southern Home: or, The South and Its People.* Boston: A.G. Brown and Co., 1880.

Secondary Sources

Allen, Richard. *The Life, Experience, and Gospel Labors of the Rt. Reverend Richard Allen.* New York: Abingdon Press, 1960.

Allport, Gordon W. *The Nature of Prejudice.* New York; Doubleday and Company, Inc., 1958.

Aptheker, Herbert. *American Negro Slave Revolts.* New York: Columbia University Press, 1943.

_____. (ed.). *A Documentary History of the Negro People in the United States.* 1951

_____. *The Negro in the Abolitionist Movement.* New York: International Publishers, 1940.

_____. *The Negro People in America.* New York: International Publishers, 1946.

_____. *"One Continual Cry": David Walker's Appeal to the Colored Citizens of the World (1829-1830).* New York: Humanities Press, 1915.

Armistead, Wilson. *Tribute for the Negro.* London: Charles Gilpin, 1848.

Auer, J. Jeffery (ed.). *Anti Slavery and Disunion.* 1858-1861. New York: Harper and Row, 1963.

Bardolph, Richard. *The Negro Vanguard.* New York: Rinehart and Company, 1959.

Bell, Howard Holman. *A Survey of the Negro Convention Movement, 1830-1861.* New York: Arno Press, 1969.

Bennett, Lerone, Jr. *Before the Mayflower: A History of the Negro in America (1619-1962).* Chicago: Johnson Publishing Company, 1962.

Berry, Mary Frances. *Black Resistance/White Law*. New York: Appleton-Century-Crafts, 1971.

Bibb, Henry. *Narrative of the Life and Adventures of Henry Bibb, An American Slave*. New York: N.P., 1819.

Blassingame, John W. *The Slave Community*. New York: Oxford University Press, 1972.

Bond, Frederick W. *The Negro and the Drama*. Washington, D.C.: Associated Publishers, 1940.

Bone, Robert A. *The Negro Novel in America*. New Haven, Connecticut: Yale University Press, 1958.

Bontempts, Arna, and Jack Conroy. *They Seek a City*. Garden City, New York: Doubleday, Doran and Co., 1945.

Bontempts, Arna. *Story of the Negro*. New York: Alfred A. Knopf, 1948.

Bragg, George F. *Richard Allen and Absalom Jones*, 1915.

Brawley, Benjamin Griffith (ed.). *Early Negro American Writers*. Chapel Hill: University of North Carolina Press, 1935.

Brawley, Benjamin Griffith. *The Negro in Literature and Art*. New York: Guffield and Company, 1918.

_____. *A Social History of the American Negro*. New York: The Macmillan Co., 1921.

_____. *Negro Builders and Heroes*. Chapel Hill, North Carolina: University of North Carolina Press, 1937.

_____. *The Negro Genius: A New Appraisal of the Achievement of the American Negro in Literature and the Fine Arts*. New York: Dodd, Mead and Co., 1937.

_____. *Negro Poetry and Drama*. Washington, D.C.: Associates in Negro Fold Education, 1937.

Brown, Herbert Ross. *The Sentimental Novel in America, 1789-1860*. Durham, North Carolina: Duke University Press, 1940.

Brown, Josephine. *Biography of an American Bondman*. Boston: R. F. Wallcut, 1856.

Brown, Sterling. *The Negro in American Fiction*. New York: Atheneum, 1969.

Brown, Sterling, Arthur P. Davis and Ulysses Lee, eds. *The Negro Caravan*. New York: Dryden Press, 1941.

Brown, William Wells. *Narrative of William W. Brown, a Fugitive Slave*. The Anti Slavery Office, 1847.

Carrall, Joseph Cephas. *Slave Insurrections in the United States, 1800-1865*. Boston: Chapman and Grimes, 1938.

Catterall, Helen T. (ed.). *Judicial Cases Concerning American Slavery and the Negro*. 5 Vols. Washington, D.C.: Carnegie Institution of Washington, 1926-37.

Chapman, Abraham. *The Negro in American Literature and a Bibliography of Literature By and About Negroes*. Oshkosh, Wisconsin: Wisconsin Counsel of Teachers of English, 1966.

Cromwell, John W. *The Early Convention Movement*. Washington, D.C.: American Negro Academy, 1904.

_____. *The Negro in American History*. Washington, D.C.: American Negro Academy, 1914.

Crummell, Alexander. *Africa and America*. Springfield, Massachusetts: Willey and Co., 1891.

_____. *The Man, The Negro, The Christian, A Eulogy Delivered in New York City*. New York: Egbert, Hovey and King, 1847.

_____. *The Shades and the Lights of a Fifty Years' Ministry*. N.P., 1894.

Deane, Charles. *Memoirs of George Livermore*. Cambridge: John Wilson and Son, 1869.

Detweiler, Frederick G. *The Negro Press in the United States*. 1922.

Dew, R. Thomas. *An Essay on Slavery*. Richmond: J.W. Randolph, 121 Main Street, 1849.

Douglass, Frederick. *Narrative of the Life of Frederick Douglass, An American Slave.* Published at the Anti-Slavery Office, No. 25 Cornhill, 1845.

Drotning, Phillip T. *Black Heroes in Our Nation's History: A Tribute to Those Who Helped Shape America.* New York: Cowles Book Co., 1969.

Dubois, William E. Brughardt. *A Selected Bibliography of the Negro in America.* Atlanta: Atlanta University Press, 1905.

_____. *Black Folk Then and Now.* New York: Henry Holt and Co., 1939.

_____. *Black Reconstruction in America 1860-1880.* New York: Atheneum, 1972.

_____ and Guy B. Johnson. *Encyclopedia of the Negro: Preparatory Volume.* Revised and Enlarged. New York: Phelps-Stokes Ford, 1946.

_____. *The Gift of the Black Folk: The Negroes in the Making of America.* Boston: Stratford Co., 1924.

_____. *The Negro Church.* Atlanta: Atlanta University Press, 1903.

_____. *The Suppression of the African Slave Trade, 1683-1820.* Cambridge: Harvard University Press, 1904.

Eaton, Clement. *The Growth of Southern Civilization 1790-1860.* New York: Harper and Row, Publishers, 1961.

Evans, Maurice S. *Black and White in the Southern States.* New York: Longmans, Green and Co., 1915.

Farrison, William Edward. *William Wells Brown, Author and Reformer.* Chicago: University Press, 1969.

Fauset, Arthur H. *Sojourner Truth, God's Faithful Pilgrim.* Chapel Hill: University of North Carolina Press, 1944.

Feldstein, Stanley. *Once a Slave: The Slaves' View of Slavery*. New York: William and Co., 1971.

Foner, Phillip S. *The Life and Writings of Frederick Douglass*. 4 Vols. New York: International Publishers, 1950-55.

Franklin, John Hope. *From Slavery to Freedom: A History of Negro Americans*. New York: Alfred A. Knopf, 1947.

_____. *The Free Negro in North Carolina, 1790-1860*. Chapel Hill: University of North Carolina Press, 1943.

_____. *The Militant South, 1800-1861*. Cambridge, Massachusetts: Belknap Press of Harvard University Press, 1956.

Frazier, Edward Franklin. *The Negro Church in America*. Liverpool, England: Liverpool University Press, 1964.

_____. *The Negro in the United States*. New York: Macmillan Co., 1949.

Fuller, Louis. *The Crusade Against Slavery 1830-1860*. New York: Harper and Brothers, 1960.

Gaines, Francis Pendleton. *The Southern Plantation: A Study in the Development and Accuracy of Tradition*. New York: Columbia University Press, 1924.

Gara, Larry. *The Liberty Line: The Legend of the Underground Railroad*. Lexington: University of Kentucky Press, 1961.

_____. *The Negroes' Civil War: How American Negroes Felt and Acted During the War for the Union*. New York: Pantheon Books, 1965.

Garrett, Romeo B. *Famous First Facts About Negroes*. New York: Arno Press, 1972.

Garrison, William Lloyd. *An Address Delivered Before the Free People of Color in Philadelphia*. New York and Other Cities: 1831.

Garrison, William Lloyd. *Thoughts in African Colonization, or An Imparted Exhibition Doctrine, Principles and Purpose of the American Colonization Society.* Boston: Knapp and Garrison, 1832.

Genovese, Eugene D. *Roll, Jordan, Roll.* New York: Pantheon Book, 1947.

Gilbert, Alice. *Narrative of Sojourner Truth.* Boston: By the Author, 1875.

Gloster, Hugh M. *Negro Voices in American Fiction.* Chapel Hill: University of North Carolina Press, 1948.

Gloucester, S.H. A Discourse Delivered on the Occasion of the Death of Mr. James Forten, N.P., 1842.

Goldstein, Robert. *The Negro Revolution.* New York: Macmillan Co., 1968.

Gosnell, Harold Foote. *Negro Politicians.* Chicago: University of Chicago Press, 1935.

Grace, Greenwood. *Poems.* Boston: Ticknor, Reed, and Fields, 1850.

Graham, Shirley. *There Was Once a Slave.* New York: Julius Messner, 1951.

Greene, Lorenzo Johnson. *The Negro in Colonial New England, 1620-1776.* New York: Columbia University Press, 1942.

Griffiths, Julia (ed.). *Autographs for Freedom.* Cleveland: Jewett, Proctor, and Worthington, 1853.

Gross, Bella. *Clarion Call: The History and Development of the Negro People's Convention Movement in the United States from 1817 to 1840.* New York: By the Author, 1947.

Halass, Nicholas. *The Rattling Chains.* New York: David McKay Co., 1966.

Hatcher, William Eldridge. *John Jasper, the Unmatched Negro Philosopher and Preacher.* New York: Fleming H. Revell Co., 1908.

Heermance, J. Noel. *William Wells Brown and Clotelle: A Portrait of the Artist in the First Negro Novel*. Hamden, Connecticut: Shoe String Press, 1969.

Herbert, Hilary Abner. *Abolition Crusade and its Consequences*. New York: Scribner, 1912.

Hesseltine, William Best. *The South in American History*. New York: Prentice-Hall, 1949.

Holland, Frederic May. *Frederick Douglass: The Colored Orator*. New York: Funk and Wagnalls Co., 1891.

Holly, James T. *A Vindication of the Capacity of the Negro Race for Self-Government and Colored Progress*. New Haven: W.H. Stanley, 1857.

Hopkins, Joseph G.E., ed. *Concise Dictionary of American Biography*. New York: Charles Scribner's Sons, 1964.

Hort, Albert B. *Slavery and Abolition, 1831-1841*. New York: Harper and Brothers, 1906.

Hughes, Carl Milton. *The Negro Novelist, A Discussion of the Writings of American Negro Novelists 1940-1950*. New York: Citadel Press, 1953.

Hughes, Langston. *Famous American Negroes*. New York: Dodd, Mead and Co., 1954.

Hume, John Ferguson. *The Abolitionists: Together With Personal Memories of the Struggle for Human Rights, 1830-1864*. New York: G.P. Putnam's Son, 1905.

Hyde, William. *Encyclopaedia of the History of St. Louis*, (Vol, III), 1899.

Jackson, Ruther Porter. *Free Negro Labor and Property Holding in Virginia, 1830-1860*. New York: D. Appleton-Century Co., 1942.

Jenkins, William S. *Pro-Slavery Thought in the Old South*, Chapel Hill: N.P., 1935.

Johnson, Oliver. *William Lloyd Garrison and His Times*. Boston: B.B. Russell and Co., 1880.

Johnston, Ruby F. *The Development of Negro Religion*. New York: Philosophical Library, 1954.

Jones, Absalom. *A Thanksgiving Sermon Preached January 1, 1808, in St. Thomas' or the African Episcopal Church, Philadelphia*. Philadelphia: By the Author.

Katz, William Loren. *Eyewitness: The Negro in American History*. New York: Pitman Publishing Co., 1967.

Kunitz, Stanley J., and Howard Haycraft. *American Authors 1600-1900: A Biographical Dictionary of American Literature*. New York: H.W. Wilson Co., 1938.

Lincoln, E. Eric. *The Negro Pilgrimage in America: The Coming of Age of Black Americans*. New York: Frederick A. Praeger, 1969.

Litwack, Leon F. *North of Slavery: The Negro in the Free States, 1790-1860*. Chicago: The University of Chicago Press, 1961.

Lloyd, Arthur Y. *The Slavery Controversy, 1831-1860*. Chapel Hill: University of North Carolina Press, 1939.

Locke, Mary S. *Anti-Slavery in America*. Boston: Ginn and Co., 1901.

Loggin, Vernon. *The Negro Author, His Development in America*. New York: Columbia University Press, 1931.

Long, Richard A. and Collier, Eugenia W., eds. *American Writing: An Anthology of Prose and Poetry*. New York: New York University Press, 1972.

Lovejoy, Joseph C. and Owen. *Memoir of the Reverend Elijah P. Lovejoy*. N.P., 1838.

Luguen, Jermain Wesley. *The Reverend J. W. Loguen as a Slave and as a Freeman*. Syracuse: J.C.K. Truair, 1859.

McPherson, James M. *The Negros' Civil War*. New York: Vintage Books, 1965.

Mary, Jesse. *The Anti-Slavery Crusade: A Chronicle of the Gathering Storm.* New Haven: Yale University Press, 1921.

Matthews, Donald G. *Slavery and Methodism.* Princeton: Princeton University Press, 1965.

May, Samuel J. *Some Recollections of our Anti-Slavery Conflict.* Boston: Field, Osgood and Company, 1869.

Mays, Benjamin, and Nicholson, Joseph William. *The Negro's Church.* New York: Institute of Social and Religious Research, 1933.

Meir, August. *Negro Thought in America, 1880-1915.* Ann Arbor: University of Michigan Press, 1963.

Meltzer, Milton. *In Their Own Words: A History of the American Negro 1619-1865.* New York: Thomas Y. Crowell Co., 1964.

Miller, Kelly. *Race Adjustment Essays in the Negro in America.* New York: Neale Publishing Co., 1908.

Miller, Marion Mills. *American Debate.* New York: G.P. Putnam's Sons, 1916.

Mitchell, Loften. *Black Drama: The Story of the American Negro in the Theatre.* New York: Hawthorne Books, 1967.

Myrdal, Gunnar. *An American Dilemma.* New York: Harper and Brothers, 1944.

Nell, William C. *The Colored Patriots of American Revolution.* Boston: F. C. Wallcut, 1855.

Nelson, John Herbert. *The Negro Character in American Literature.* Laurence, Kansas: Department of Journalism Press, 1926.

Newsome, Albert Ray, ed. *Studies in History and Political Science.* Chapel Hill: University of North Carolina Press, 1947.

Nichols, Charles Harold. *Many Thousand Gone: The Ex-slaves' account of their Bondage and Freedom.* Leiden, Netherlands: E.J. Brill, 1963.

Nichols, Charles Harold, ed. Black Men in Chains: Narratives by Escaped Slaves. New York: Lawrence Hill and Co., 1972.

Northrup, Solomon. Twelve Years a Slave. Auburn, New York: Derby and Miller, 1853.

Olmstead, Frederick Law. The Cotton Kingdom. 2 Vols. New York: Mason and Brothers, 1861.

_____. A Journey in the Back Country in the Winter of 1853-1854. 2 Vol.s New York: G.P. Putnam's Sons, 1901.

Ottley, Roi. Black Odyssey: The Story of the Negro in America. London: John Murray, 1949.

Parrott, Russell. An Address on the Abolition of the Slave Trade, Delivered January 1, 1816. Philadelphia: By The Author, 1816.

Pauli, Hertha. Her Name was Sojourner Truth. New York: Appleton-Century-Crofts, 1962.

Payne, Daniel A. History of the African Methodist Episcopal Church. Nashville: African Methodist Episcopal Sunday School Union, 1891.

_____. Recollections of Seventy Years. Nashville: African Methodist Episcopal Sunday School Union, 1888.

Penn, I. Garland. The Afro-American Press and Its Editors. Springfield, Massachusetts: Willey and Co., 1891.

Pennington, James W. C. An Address at Hartford, August 1, 1856, N.P., n.d.

_____. The Fugitive Blacksmith. London: C. Gilpin, 1850.

_____. A Textbook of the Origin and History of the Colored People. Hartford, Connecticut: L. Skinner, 1841.

Phillips, Ulrich Bonnell. American Negro Slavery. New York: G. W. Dillingham Co., 1900.

Pickard, Katie E. The Kidnapped and the Ransomed. New York: Negro Publication Society of America, 1941.

Pillsbury, Parker. *Acts of the Anti-Slavery Apostles.* Rochester, New York: Claque, Wegman, Schlict and Co., 1883.

Pomerantz, Sidney I. *New York, an American City, 1783-1803.* New York: Columbia University Press, 1938.

Powell, Aaron Mary. *Personal Reminiscences of the Anti-Slavery Reformers and Reforms.* New York: Caulon Press, 1899.

Purvis, Robert. *A Tribute to the Memory of Thomas Shipley, the Philanthropist, Delivered at St. Thomas', November 23, 1836.* Philadelphia: By the Author, 1836.

Quarles, Benjamin. *The Negro in the Civil War.* Boston: Little, Brown and Co., 1953.

────. *The Negro in the Making of America.* London: Collier-Macmillan, 1964.

────. *Black Abolitionists.* New York: Oxford University Press, 1969.

Redding, J. Saunders. *To Make A Poet Black.* Chapel Hill, North Carolina: University of North Carolina Press, 1939.

────. *They Came in Chains: Americans from Africa.* Philadelphia: J.B. Lippincott Co., 1950.

────. *The Lonesome Road: The Story of the Negro's Part In America.* Garden City, New York: Doubleday and Co., 1958.

Reuter, Edward Byron. *The Mulatto in the United States.* Richard G. Badger, 1918.

Rue, C. Duncan. *The Rise and Fall of Black Slavery.* New York: Harper and Row, 1975.

Rollin, Frank A. *Life and Public Services of Martin R. Delany.* Boston: Lee and Shepard, 1868.

Rose, Arnold Marshall. *The Negro in America.* New York: Harper and Row, 1964.

Ruchames, Louis. *The Abolitionists: a Collection of their writings.* New York: Putnam, 1963.

Schraufnagel, Noel. From Apology to Protest: The Black American Novel. Deland, Florida: Everett/Edwards, 1973.

Siebert, Wilbur H. The Underground Railroad From Slavery to Freedom. New York: The Macmillan Co., 1898.

Silberman, Charles E. Crisis in Black and White. New York: Vintage Books, 1964.

Simmons, William J. Men of Mark: Eminent, Progressive and Rising. Cleveland: George M. Rewell and Co., 1887.

Smith, H. Shelton. In His Image, But..Racism in Southern Religion. Durham: Duke University Press, 1972.

Smith, Shelton, Handy, Robert T., Loetscher, Ceffert A. eds. American Christianity: An Historical Interpretation with Representative Documents. 2 Vols. New York: Charles Scribner's Sons, 1960-63.

Smith, William A. Lectures on the Philosophy and Practice of Slavery. Nashville: n.p., 1856.

Stamp, Kenneth M. The Era of Reconstruction 1865-1877. New York: Vintage Books, 1965.

Starobin, Robert S. Industrial Slavery in the Old South. New York: Oxford University Press, 1970.

Stanton, William R. The Leopard's Spot: Scientific Attitudes Toward Race in America, 1815-59. Chicago: n.p. 1960.

Sunderland, LeRoy. Anti-Slavery Manual. New York: S.W. Benedict Co., 1837.

Swift, Lindsay. William Lloyd Garrison. Philadelphia: George W. Jacobs and Co., 1911.

Tannenbaum, Frank. Slave and Citizen. New York: Alfred A. Knopf, 1947.

Tanner, Henry. *History of the Rise and Progress of Alton Riots*, n.p. 1878.

Thomas, John L., ed. *Slavery Attacked: The Abolitionist Crusade*. Englewood Cliffs, New Jersey: Prentice-Hall, 1965.

Thorpe, Earl E. *Black Historians: A Critique*. New York: William Morrow and Co., 1971.

_____. *The Mind of the Negro: An Intellectual History of Afro-Americans*. Baton Rouge: Ortlieb Press, 1961.

Tocqueville, Alexis de. *Democracy in America*. 2 Vols. New York: Phillips Braley, 1945.

Truth, Sojourner. *Narrative of Sojourner Truth*. Boston: J.B. Herrington and Son, 1850.

Turner, Edward Raymond. *The Negro in Pennsylvania*. Washington, D.C.: American Historical Association, 1911.

Tyler, Alice Felt. *Freedom's Ferment.* New York: Harper and Row, 1944.

Van Deusen, John G. *The Black Man in White America.* Washington, D.C.: Associated Publishers, 1944.

Ward, Samuel Ringgold. *The Autobiography of a Fugitive Negro*. New York: Arno Press, 1968.

Wesley, Charles Harris. *The History of the Prince Hall Grand Lodge.* Wilberforce, Ohio: Central State College Press, 1961.

Wesley, Charles H., and Romero, Patricia W. *Negro Americans in the Civil War: From Slavery to Citizenship*. New York: Publishers Co., 1968.

Whiteman, Maxwell. *A Century of Fiction by American Negroes*. Philadelphia: Maurice Jacobs, 1955.

Whitlow, Roger. *Black American Literature: A Critical History*. Chicago: Nelson Hall, 1973.

Wigham, Eliza. *The Anti-Slavery Cause in America: Its Martyrs*. London: A. W. Bennett, 1863.

Williams, George W. The History of the Negro Race in America, from 1619 to 1880. New York: G.P. Putnam's Sons, 1883.

Williams, Kenny J. They Also Spoke: An Essay on Negro Literature in America, 1787-1930. Nashville, Tennessee: Townsend Press, 1970.

Willey, Austin. The History of the Anti-Slavery Cause in State and Nation. Portland, Maine: Brown Thurston and Hoyt, Flagg and Stonham, 1886.

Woodson, Carter G. The Education of the Negro Prior to 1861. 2nd ed. Washington, D.C.: Associated Publishers, 1919.

_____. The History of the Negro Church. Washington, D. C.: Associated Publishers, 1921.

_____. The Negro in Our History. Washington, D.C.: Associated Publishers, 1922.

_____. and Wesley, Charles H. The Negro in Our History. 10th ed. Washington, D.C.: Associated Publishers, 1947.

_____., ed. The Mind of the Negro as Reflected in Letters Written During the Crisis 1800-1860. Washington, D.C.: Association for the Study of Negro Life and History, 1926.

_____, and Wesley, Charles H. Negro Maker of History. Washington, D.C.: Associated Publishers, 1928.

_____. The Negro Professional Man and the Community with Special Emphasis on the Physician and the Lawyer. Washington, D.C.: Association for the Study of Negro Life and History, 1934.

_____. The African Background Outline Or Handbook for the Study of the Negro. Washington, D.C.: Association for the Study of Negro Life and History, 1930.

_____. Negro Orators and Their Orations. Washington, D.C.: Associated Publishers, 1925.

_____. Negro Makers of History. 5th ed., revised. Washington, D.C.: Associated Publishers, 1958.

Work, Monroe. <u>Bibliography of the Negro in Africa and America</u>. New York: H.W. Wilson Company, 1928.

Wright, Lyle H. <u>American Friction 1851-1875: A Contribution Toward a Bibliography</u>. San Marino, California: Hutington Library, 1957.

Wright, James Martin. <u>The Free Negro in Maryland. 1634-1860</u>. New York: Columbia University Press, 1921.

Yellin, Jean Fagan. <u>The Intricate Knot: Black Figures in American Literature, 1776-1863</u>. New York: New York University Press, 1972.

Articles

Abdul, Raoul. "The Negro Playwright on Broadway," in <u>Anthology of the American Negro in the Theatre</u>. Edited by Lindsay Patterson. New York: Publishers Co., 1967, pp. 59-63.

Abramson, Doris M. "William Wells Brown: America's First Negro Playwright." <u>Educational Theatre Journal</u>, October 20, 1968, pp. 370-75.

Aptheker, Herbert. "The Negro in the Abolitionist Movement." <u>Science and Society</u>, Vol. 5 (1941), pp. 2-23, 146-172.

Baker, Henry E. "Benjamin Banneker, the Negro Mathematician and Astronomer." <u>Journal of Negro History</u>, Vol. 3 (April 1918), pp. 99-118.

Bardolph, Richard. "The Distinguished Negro in America 1770-1939." <u>American Historical Review</u>, Vol. 60, (April 1955), pp. 527-547.

Bell, Bernard W. "Literary Sources of the Early Afro-American Novel." <u>College Language Association Journal</u>, 18 (September) 1974, pp. 24-34.

Bell, Howard H. "National Negro Conventions of the Middle 1840's: Moral Suasion vs. Political Action." <u>Journal of Negro History</u>, 42 (October) 1957, pp. 247-260.

Bell, Howard H. "Negro Nationalism: A Factor in Emigration Projects, 1858-1861." *Journal of Negro History*, 47 (January), 1962, pp. 42-53.

Bontemps, Arna. "The Negro Contribution to American Letters" in *The American Negro Reference Book*. Edited by John P. Davis, Englewood Cliffs, New Jersey: Prentice-Hall, 1966, pp. 851-78.

Braithwaite, William S. "Alain Locke's Relationship to the Negro in American Literature." *Phylon*, 18 (Second Quarter), 1957, pp. 163-73.

Brewer, W.M. "Henry Highland Garnet," *Journal of Negro History*, Vol. 7 (January 1922), pp. 11-22.

Brown, Sterling A. "The American Race Problem as Reflected in American Literature." *Journal of Negro Education*, 8 (July 1, 1939).

Bullock, Penelope. "The Mulatto in American Fiction." *Phylon*, 6 (First Quarter), 1945, pp. 78-82.

Chandler, G. Lewis. "Coming of Age: A Note on American Negro Novelists." *Phylon*, 7 (first Quarter), 1948, pp. 25-29.

Channing, William Ellery. "The African Character," in John A. Collins (ed.), *The Anti Slavery Redneck*. Boston: n.p., 1842.

Coleman, E.M. "William Wells Brown As An Historian." *Journal of Negro History*, January 31, 1946, pp. 47-59.

Cromwell, John W. "The Aftermath of the Nat Turner's Insurrection." *Journal of Negro History*, Vol. 5 (April 1920), pp. 208-224.

Davis, John W. "George Liele and Andrew Bryan, Pioneer Negro Baptist Preachers." *Journal of Negro History* Vol. 3 April 1918, pp. 119-127.

Dubois, W.E.B. "Strivings of the Negro People," *Atlantic Monthly*, LXXX (August 1897), pp. 194-195.

Farrison, William E. "William Wells Brown in Buffalo." *Journal of Negro History*, Vol. 39 (July 1954), pp. 298-314.

Farrison, William E. "William Wells Brown, Sound Reformer." *Journal of Negro Education*, 18 (Winter), 1949, pp. 29-39.

―――――. "Phylon Profile XVI, William Wells Brown." *Phylon* 9 (First Quarter), 1948, pp. 13-23.

Hopkins, Pauline E. "William Wells Brown." *Colored American Magazine*, 2 (January) 1901, pp. 232-36.

Johnson, Guy B. "Negro Racial Movements in the United States," *The American Journal of Sociobiology*, Vol. 93 (July 1937), pp. 57-71.

Litwack, Leon F. "The Emancipation of the Negro Abolitionist," *The Anti-Slavery Vanguard*. Edited by Martin Duberman. Princeton: Princeton University Press, 1965, pp. 395-417.

London, Fred. "Henry Bibb, A Colonizer." *Journal of Negro History*, October 1920, pp. 437-447.

Nichols, Charles H., Jr. "Slave Narratives and Plantation Legend." *Phylon* 10 (Third Quarter), 1949, pp. 201-209.

Perlman, Daniel. "Organization of the Free Negro in New York City, 1800-1860." *Journal of Negro History* 56, July 1971, pp. 181-197.

Quarles, Benjamin. "Minister Without Portfolio." *Journal of Negro History* 39 (January), 1957, pp. 27-42.

Smith, Robert P. "William Cooper Nell: Crusading Black Abolitionist." *Journal of Negro History* 55 (July), 1970, pp. 182-99.

Wesley, Charles H. "Creating and Maintaining an Historical Tradition." *Journal of Negro History* 49 (January), 1964, pp. 13-33.

―――――. "The Participation of Negroes in Anti Slavery Political Parties." *Journal of Negro History* 29 (January), 1944, pp. 32-74.

―――――. "Negro Suffrage in the Period of Constitution-Making, 1787-1865." *Journal of Negro History* 32 (April), 1947, pp. 143-68.

Newspapers

Albany, New York, The Northern Star and Freedom's Advocate. February 2, 1842 - January 2, 1843 (irregular).

Baltimore, Weekly Sun. June 9, 1860.

Boston, The Abolitionist. 1833.

Boston, Emancipator and Republican (title varies). May 4, 1833 - June 30, 1835; August 1835 - June 1836; April 23, 1836 - December 26, 1850.

Boston, Liberator. 1831-1865.

Cleveland, The Alienated American. April 9, 1853.

Jonesboro, Tennessee, Emancipator (reprint). Nashville, Tennessee: B. H. Murphy, 1932.

New York, Anti-Slavery Record. 1835-1837.

New York, Anti-Slavery Reporter. 1833.

New York, Colored American. January 7, 1837 - November 23, 1839; March 14, 1840 - March 13, 1841.

New York, Freedom's Journal. March 27, 1827 - March 28, 1829.

New York, Human Rights. September 1836.

New York, The National Anti-Slavery Standard. May 31, 1849 - May 15, 1851.

New York, Ram's Horn. November 5, 1847.

New York, The Rights of All. 1829 (irregular).

New York, Slave's Friend. 1836 - 1838.

New York, Weekly Advocate. 1836.

New York, The Weekly Anglo-African. July 23, 1859 - July 14, 1860.

Rochester, New York, The North Star (also Frederick
    Douglass' Paper). 1842-1858.

San Francisco, Mirror of the Times. December 12, 1857.

INDEX

Abolition	24
African Methodist Episcopal Zion Church	35
Allen, Reverend Richard	34-35
American Anti-Slavery Society	30
American Colonization Society	32,78
American Fugitive in Europe	18
American Peace Society	18
Anglocization	5
Anti-Slavery Society	27,78-79
Anti-Slavery Society of Western New York	17
Armistead, Wilson	20
Attainment of Black Civilization	23
Baranger, Pierce Jean de	19
Battle of Miliken Bend	39
Battle of Poison Springs	41
Bibb, Henry	25,50
Big House	2
Biography of an American Bondman	1
Birney, James G.	33
Black Daniel Webster	27
Black Man, The,	22-25,35,72
Black Soldiers	40
Boston Public School Segregation	26
Boyer	28
British West Indies	30
Brown, John	41
Brown, Josephine	1
Brown, William	35
Brown, William Wells,	6-7,10-11,16,27
ancestry, 4; beating, 3	
Burns, Jabez	21
Callioux, Capt. Andre	41
Canada	15,18
Carmichael, Stokeley	60
Channing, William Ellery	79
Christophe, Henri	28
Christy, Major William	7
Civil Rights Bill	44
Cliometric School	4
Clotel	45-50
Colburn, James	7
Colonization	24
Confederacy	6
Confederate Emancipation Proclamation	6

Cook overseer	3
Cotton gin	37
Craft, William	20
Crandall, Prudence	23-33,37
Crummel, Alexander	20
Cuba	29
Desalines	28
Democratic instrument of torture	18
Dickens, Charles	47
Douglass, Frederick	1,26-27,38,43,72
Douglass, L.H.	43
Downing, George T.	43
Dred Scott Decision	34,78
Dummer, Governor	31
Edinburgh Ladies Emancipation Society	20
Eliza	47
Elizabeth (Brown's mother)	1
Emancipation Proclamation	38,44,59,79
Confererate, 6	
England	20
Enterprise, USS	8,11
Escape, The	51-56
Escape to Canada	12,15
Fairbanks, Reverend Calvin	36
Farmer, William	21
Female Anti-Slavery Society of Salem	77
Field niggers	2
Fogel, Robert W.	4
Freeland, Major	6,7
Friends, The (see Quakers)	16
Fugitive Slave Law	64
Gag Law	34
Garnet, Henry Alexander	27
Garrison, William Lloyd	19,26,32,33,60,65,70,79
Genius of Universal Emancipation	17
Haskel, Friend	5-6, 8
Hayden, Lewis	36
Higgins, George	1
Higginson, Col. T.W.	39-40
House niggers	2
Hugo, Victor	19
Hunter, Maj. Gen.	40
Iron Collar	18

Jackson, Andrew	43
Jacobs, Francis	35
Jamaica	29
Jefferson, Thomas	45-46
John (see Patsey)	7
Johnson, Andrew	42-44
Josephine (Brown's daughter)	1
King, Martin Luther, Jr.	60
Ku Klux Klan	57
Ladies Anti-Slavery Society	33
Lake Erie Steamboat	16-17
Latin American Slavery	29
Liberator	17,26,32
Lincoln, Abraham	79
Livermore, George	36
Loguen, Jermin W.	36
Lovejoy, Elijah P.	33
Lovejoy incident	8
Lundy, Benjamin	31
Malcolm X	60
Mason and Dixon Line	39
Medical training of Brown	8-9
Militancy	21,64
Miller, William	35
Montgomery, James	20
Moral Persuasion	21
Narratives,	63
National Era	26
Negro in the American Rebellion, The	36
Negro car	19
Negro pew	19,34
Negro whipping post	44
Negro worship	35
Nell, William C.	26
New militancy	21,64
News media attack	23
New York State Anti-Slavery Society	33
Nice child play	19
North Star	26
Ohio	15
Oliver Twist	42
Paris Peace Conference	18-19
Patsey	7
Paul, St.	43

Peculiar customs	14
People's poet	19
Pennington, James W. C.	27
Petion	28
Phillips, Wendell	27,33,70
Placido	29
Plymouth Rock	30
Price, Enoch	13
Price, Mrs. E.	14
Pro-Slavery Americans	19
Propaganda, Slaveholders	67
Quakers	15,31
Racialized consciousness	4
Randall, slave	3,70
Rising Son	35
Ruggles, David	36
Sabbath for slaves	10
Sandford	2,16
Santo Domingo slavery	28
Shakespeare's Othellian World	5
Sharp, Samuel	29
Slave marriages	14
Slave quarters	3
Slave rebellions	31
Smith, Elijah W.	27
Smith, James M'Cune	27,76
Smith, R.	21
Smoke house	7
Society of Friends (see Quakers)	31
Southern Rights Convention	24
Stevenson, John	21
Stowe, Harriet Beecher	26
Sumner, Charles	50
Sumter, Fort	37
Tailor, Willis	13
Taney, Roger	2
Tappan, Lewis	72
Tarry, Charles T.	34
Thompson, George	19,21
Three years in Europe	18
Thoughts on African Colonization	32
Tocqueville, Alexis de	19,65-66,80
Toussaint, L'Ouverture	28
Tribute to the Negro, A.	20

<u>Uncle Tom's Cabin</u>	26,50
<u>Underground railroad</u>	36
Virginia play	7
<u>Voice of Freedom</u>	26
Walker, David	33
Walker, James	1,6,11-12,45
Ward, Samuel Ringgold	26-27
Webster, Delia A.	36
Weld, Theodore	70
Wells, William	16
West Indies Brethren	21
Whitney, Eli	37
Whipper, William	43
Young, Dr. John	2-3,10-13,63

Author's Biographical Note

Love Henry Whelchel, Jr. is a native of Warren County, Georgia. He graduated from Paine College, Augusta, Georgia with the A.B. degree in 1959. He graduated from Boston University School of Theology, Boston, Massachusetts with the S.T.B. degree in 1962. He graduated from New York University in New York City with the M.A. degree in 1963. He attended Duke University, Durham, North Carolina and graduated with the Ph.D. degree in 1981. He taught at Miles College and pastored Metropolitan Christian Methodist Episcopal Church from 1963 to 1969. He served as the minister of the Russell Memorial Christian Methodist Episcopal Church in Durham, North Carolina from 1969 to 1982. He is presently serving as the minister of Phillips Temple Christian Methodist Episcopal Church, Dayton, Ohio.